More Miniature Merchant Ships

The New Guide to Waterline Ship Modelling in 1/1200 Scale

—

John Bowen

CONWAY MARITIME PRESS

Text copyright © John Bowen, 2003
Volume copyright © Conway Maritime Press, 2003

First published in Great Britain in 2003 by Conway Maritime Press,
The Chrysalis Building, Bramley Road, LONDON W10 6SP
www.conwaymaritime.com

Distributed in North America by Casemate, 2114 Darby Road, Haverton, PA 19083

A member of **Chrysalis** Books plc

British Library Cataloguing in Publication Data
A record for this title is available upon request from the British Library

ISBN 0 85177 936 0

All photographs by the author or from the author's collection unless otherwise stated.

Designed by Stephen Dent
Printed and Bound in Spain

Contents

Part I: Construction Compendium
An A–Z of tools and processes used by the miniature modeller

Part II: Ship Model Plans

The Hamburg-Amerika liner *Deutschland* of 1900

Introduction

This book is an extension to my previous title *Miniature Merchant Ships* (published by Conway in 1997). It contains a further selection of the plans that I have drawn during the past 25 years or so, for the construction of 1/1200-scale waterline models. Because the plans have been produced over a period of years, there are some variations in layout and in the amount of detail included; the majority have been based on prints of the shipbuilder's original plans or, if not available, published authentic material. In general they show the ship as completed – almost invariably its best configuration. For this reason some changes in appearance and visible detail may be noticed when compared with photographs taken during the course of a vessel's life, the result of subsequent overhauls and alterations. The techniques and materials that I have found satisfactory for building these miniatures were described in the earlier work, which is currently being reprinted; I have taken the opportunity to present the essentials in a different manner. However, for the sake of continuity and sense, a small number of diagrams from the earlier work have been included here.

Two questions are frequently put to me: 'why a miniature model?' and 'why do you prefer this form of modelling?' In response to the first question, one of the attractions of the miniature is that it is possible to capture the appearance of a vessel in a model only a few inches long. But it does require patience, craftsmanship and strict adherence to scale to produce a satisfactory result. Another virtue of a miniature is that it needs only a small working area and a relatively modest tool kit, and the finished product occupies only a modicum of space. Turning now to the second question, I must ask for some forbearance; to explain it means going back to

boyhood. I had, from a very early age, an interest in small craft such as fishing boats, sailing barges and Dutch coasters, through living in a small, southeast-coast harbour town. At school a number of us – we must have been around 10 years old at the time – had been making small block models of racing cars and aeroplanes. It was when a copy of Bassett-Lowke's catalogue of ship models and their fittings came into my hands that my interest turned to (and has remained with) 'steamers' – powered merchant ships – and warships.

My first attempt at these kinds of vessel was a waterline model of a tug, some 3in long (I know its size because I still have it), based on a photograph of a working model of one in the Bassett-Lowke catalogue. This was followed by very small models of destroyers and sundry other warships and merchant ships. A term later one of the group came back with a Bassett-Lowke 1/1200-scale waterline model of the Union-Castle liner *Arundel Castle*. I decided to try to make a copy of it, as far as an 11 year old with but a penknife, a pair of milliner's pliers, some wood, pins, card and a few tins of enamel paint, plus the restrictions of a preparatory boarding school, could manage. This model is shown in on page 7 (Photo 7). Over the years some more models, still miniatures, were built, poster paints having replaced the enamels. Sometime in the early 1930s more interest was created with the acquisition of a copy of Talbot-Booth's newly published book *Waterline Ship Models*. It was about this time that I came across a technical journal, *The Motor Ship*, which proved to be a good source of plans for many types of ships. More miniatures followed, but still without a great deal of detail. Then came the war, and when it was over 1/1200-scale modelling was resumed; the rest is history. The Bibby liner

1 The Blue Star Line cargo ship *English Star.*

2 The almost completed model of the Greek tanker *Tina Onassis* (1953)

3 The Canadian Pacific cargo ship *Beavercove*, built in 1946 by the Fairfield Shipbuilding & Engineering Co Ltd, Glasgow.

4 This little model of the German rotor ship *Barbara* is an example of the adaptability of miniatures to portray the ordinary ship types.

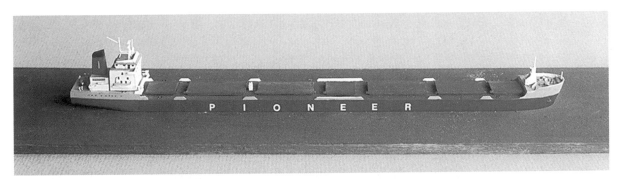

5 The large bulk-carrier *Saskatchewan Pioneer* was another product of the Fairfield yard in Glasgow, being completed in 1983 for the Pioneer Shipping Company, Canada.

6 The Bibby Line motor ship *Derbyshire*

7 The author's first 1/1200 (approx) scale waterline model, the *Arundel Castle.*

8 The completed model of Doxford Economy ship *Peebles* still on its working baseboard.

Derbyshire was the last pre-war poster-paint model, for Reeves (well-known suppliers of artists' materials) had brought out their breakaway range of paints for modelmakers in general, but aimed especially at the builders of miniature ship models. The outstanding feature of these paints was that they had excellent covering power from a very thin coat. In addition, the range included the standard shades used by several well-known shipping lines. It was reintroduced after the war, but production ceased after a few years. Fortunately paints with similar characteristics became, and are still, available from a number of manufacturers.

Some points about techniques and working practices may be of value. Cleanliness during the painting stage is all-important: every effort should be made to keep surfaces dust-free. Good lighting is necessary for close work (see Tools, p40). Attention to scale and accuracy are essential. But having said that, at this size many objects such as winches appear more as a solid mass with an individual overall shape but no visible details, so these can be represented by solid blocks with the item's characteristic outline. A number of the fittings can be made using the resin-casting process, and this can be advantageous if a quantity of an item is required. No details of this process have been included since I have not yet attempted it myself.

A frequent comment is that there are not many plans drawn full-size for 1/1200-scale models. This should not really be a deterrent. True, it is handy to be able to work from a plan reproduced full-size for a model at that scale. But if something larger is all that is available, then use it. Admittedly some modellers might find the arrival of a ship-yard plan 30in wide and 9ft long (say 75cm by almost 3m) a bit daunting, but do not be put off. Today there are readily accessible photocopying facilities capable of reducing even extra large plans. All the plans in this book are 1/1200 scale, but for those preferring to work in 1/1250 scale the plans should be reduced to 96 per cent of the printed size.

General Scenes

The following five photographs (9A–E) contain examples, or alternative examples of, a number of fittings and structural parts referred to in the individual entries in the Construction Compendium.

9A This is a fairly typical Boat Deck arrangement. The lifeboats are on chocks on the deck and are handled by quadrant davits. Alongside the funnel (note the black funnel bands) examples of mechanical ventilation units can be found, with some small cowl ventilators close by. The top on the derrick post is the type most frequently seen.

9B Points to note on this image: the heavy deck stanchions placed below each davit trackway, with a single light deck stanchion midway between each; the two boats on the left are stowed on gravity davits, but the smaller emergency lifeboat to the right is on 'Col' type davits; the curtain plates to the Boat Deck and the Promenade Deck; the full-height windows (since these two decks are wider than those below, these windows could well be done by the photocopying method described under the entry on Superstructures, see page 39).

9C This photograph of Allen Line's *Calgarian* shows a cowl-topped funnel, derrick posts with crossbar, lifeboat stowage, spacing and size of deck stanchions, cowl- and mushroom-top ventilators.

9D Here the aluminium lifeboats, on gravity davits, are fitted with canvas covers. Take note in particular of the shape and spacing of the triangular tabs to which the securing lines are attached. The deck stanchions are broad, set at an angle. The bulwark has been set inboard to form a recess in which the accommodation ladder is stowed. The deck stanchions in way are also set inboard with that section of the bulwark.

9E Photographs such as this contain much useful information for the modelmaker. On the hull note the form and shape of the hances or strengthening plating at the ends of the bridge, the position of derricks when working cargo, the deck stanchions along the open promenade deck below the boats, sundry ventilators, the layout of the open decks at the back of the bridge structure, and the proportions of the Blue Star Line's funnel colours (this was c.1936).

Part I

Construction Compendium

An A-Z of tools and processes used by the miniature modeller

Accommodation ladder

When not in use the ladder is stowed on its side in a recess on the bulwark or guardrails of the lowest open passenger deck. The recess is formed by setting the bulwark or rails inboard by about 2ft (0.61m) for just over the length of the ladder. Any deck stanchions in way are set inboard also. The ladder can be made from a narrow strip of card glued on its edge in the recess.

Adhesives

Although there is a considerable range of glues available these days not all are suitable for this kind of work. The best adhesive will be non-stringing, non-staining, colourless when dry and have a reasonable grab to allow time for final adjustments to be made. Resin W Wood Glue offers all these benefits and produces good results. Instant Glue (the kind that is very good at sticking fingers together!) has several uses in miniature modelling, both in its liquid or gel form. It is invaluable for assembling small fittings and securing derricks to derrick posts and small items to masts.

Anchors

There are two basic types of anchor found on vessels of the period covered in this book: stocked and stockless. The former was sometimes used on ships of the nineteenth and early twentieth century, where it was stowed on the fore-deck. A single radial-type davit was fitted each side to lift the anchor, when clear of the water, on to the deck. To form the anchor, tightly twist together two pieces of fine wire to create the shank, turn up the ends and cut to length. The palms are triangular in shape and can be cut from paper then glued to the end of each arm. The stock is a single piece of straight wire the same length as the shank and is pushed through the shank just below the top and at right angles to the arms.

One way to make a stockless anchor is to bend a short length of soft, fine wire into a flat-bottomed 'U' about 1mm wide and then reduce the length of each arm to about 4mm. An oval hole should be made on each side of the bow to represent the hawse hole and then, holding the 'U' in a pair of pliers with the arms resting on a piece of metal, hammer lightly to flatten the arms of the 'U' and trim to the shape of the flukes. Glue the finished 'U' to the hull with the flat of the 'U' level with the bottom of the hawse hole. Form the shank by gluing a short length of wire in the hole. At times a spare anchor was stowed on deck or vertically against the end of a deckhouse. This can be recreated by making the U-piece as above, gluing a short length of wire into the U, painting the anchor black and securing in place.

A stowed stockless anchor can be seen in the photograph of a vessel with a bar stem in the section on Hulls (see Photo 21A, p29). On some ships a recess or pocket was formed in the bow plating to allow the anchor to be stowed wholly within the line of the shell plating. An example of this can be seen in the photograph of the *Aragon* in the section on Bulwarks (see Photo 11A, p14).

Anchor cable

In practice the anchor cable is a stud link chain, which at this scale can be represented by two lengths of fine wire twisted together. Two pieces should be cut and placed between the hawse pipe opening in the deck and the windlass or cable lifters. Where a stocked anchor is shown stowed on the fore deck, a length of chain should run from the end of the shank over the ship's side to the hawse hole.

Anchor crane

The crane consists of a short robust, vertical post fitted with a derrick set at an angle of about 30 degrees by a rigid fixed span. The post can be made of a pin with fine wire for the derrick, the heel of which is attached to the post at a point 12in (0.30m) above the deck, and much finer wire for the span. The crane is fitted on the centre line of the deck forward of the windlass or cable lifters.

Bollards

The dimensions of bollards vary depending upon the size of the vessel and their position thereon. The diagram (see Fig 1) shows a casting with two round posts on a baseplate, which on a model is a rectangle of painted paper glued to the deck. The posts are short lengths of pin or fine wire set into holes made through the paper into the deck. Rather than attempt to put in pieces of wire/pin of the correct length, it is easier to put in two short lengths and then cut to the correct height with a pair of end cutters. This is an operation that must be done early on, before adjacent deck fittings are in place.

Breakwater

Situated on the weather deck forward, the breakwater comprises two lengths of plate set at an angle to the centerline and supported by a number of triangular brackets fitted on the after side. The plates rake slightly forward from the bottom. They are about 3ft (0.90m) high at the centre line, decreasing to 2ft (0.60m) at the outboard end. The end is rounded and finishes a short distance in from the edge of the deck.

Bulwarks

Unless carved integrally with the hull, bulwarks are made from a piece of mounted shaving. They should be cut with the grain of the wood horizontal (running fore and aft)

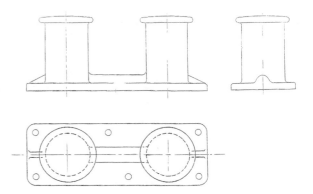

Figure 1 This shows a widely used form of bollard. The dimensions will be related to its position and use, and the size of the ship.

except when a bulwark runs around the stern or bow when the grain must be vertical. Shavings must always be fitted with the wood on the outside.

In some places short lengths of bulwark on the main hull can be glued to the edge of the deck, but generally it is better to fit them by the rebate method. To do this, cut away the top of the hull to a distance of about 1⁄16in (2mm) from the edge of the deck for the length of the bulwark. The depth of the rebate should be fractionally less than the thickness of the mounted shaving. Bulwarks have an average height of 3ft 6in to 4ft (1.07m to 1.22m), although some-

10 Two breakwaters can be seen in this photograph. Also visible are the anchor cable holders, with the cable running from hawse pipe to holder and back to the opening in the deck leading to the chain locker. The model is the Hamburg-Amerika liner *Deutschland* of 1900 at 1/1200 scale.

times more, with either a wood or steel angle bar capping. They are supported by stays spaced about 5ft (1.52m) apart, but kept clear of freeing port openings. These can be represented by very small triangles of paper glued inside the bulwarks after they have been fitted. When cutting the piece for the bulwark the depth of the rebate must be added. Where a bulwark is fitted in way of a well deck, steps have to be taken to include any upward curved part at the ends. Rather than attempt to include this with the initial cutting operation, it is better to form a small rectangle at each end (see Fig 2, centre top). Note that a shallow rebate has to be cut in the end of the erections at the ends of the well. When the glue has dried the curve at each end can be cut with the point of a new Swann Morton No 11 blade, or similar. Where there is only a short length of curved plate at the break of a forecastle, midship house or poop, insert a small square of shaving in a rebate and form the shape in the same way.

Bow bulwarks

Bow bulwarks Where there is a short spirket plate at the head of a bar stem it is better to fit this in two pieces glued to the edge of the deck and trim to shape when the glue has dried. For a vessel with either a rake or curved rolled plate (soft nose) stem and considerable flare to the bow, a short or long bulwark can be fitted by the rebate method. The expanded shape of the bulwark can be obtained as follows. Mark the end of the bulwark on the deck each side. Wrap a piece of paper round the bow so that it passes the end mark each side and projects above the deck; with thumb and forefinger press it firmly in to the flare and mark the centre line of the ship on the inside of the paper, run the pencil round the inside of the paper to mark the edge of the deck, and also mark the position of the end of the bulwark. Remove the paper and draw a line parallel to, and a scale 4ft (1.22m) above, the pencilled deck line. Draw another line parallel to and 2mm (or the depth of the rebate) below the deck line. Cut to this shape, but leave it slightly longer than the required length of the bulwark. Use this as a template to cut a bulwark from a mounted shaving, with grain running horizontally. Rather than attempt to fit the cut piece in its straight form, it can be curved by laying it on the palm of the hand and rubbing up and down its length with a cylindrical object such as a pencil, while applying a gentle pressure. When fitting in place in the rebate it is essential to ensure that the bulwark follows the flare of the bow each side and the line or curve of the stem in profile. On some ships that have a very pronounced flare, the bulwark may not follow the curve of the flare but be more upright. In such a case there will be a pronounced knuckle at the deck edge.

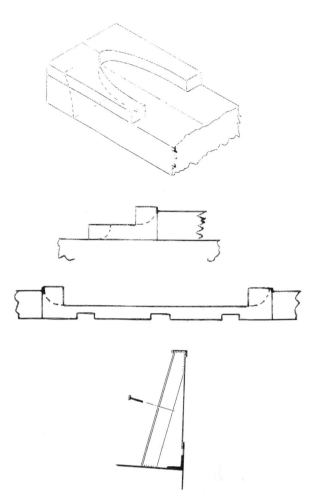

Figure 2
Above: method of forming bow bulwarks. The U-shaped piece, its thickness equal to the height of the bulwark, has been glued to the hull block. The line of the top of the bulwark should be marked on it before the hull is carved to shape. When that has been done the inside of the piece can be pared away to form a wafer thin bulwark.
Centre: The upper diagram shows hance or strengthening plate (of mounted shaving) glued to the end of house and to the edge of deck. The end glued to the house has been left over long to be trimmed later. Similarly, the end of the plate has been left square, to be trimmed to the required curve with the tip of a Swann Morton No 11 blade when the glue has dried. In the lower diagram the bulwark is fitted to the well deck. The ends have been formed as for a hance (above), with the freeing port openings cut in the bulwark section. In this diagram the bulwark is shown glued to house ends and to the edge of the deck. This is fine for a short well deck but it is better to fit a bulwark for a longer opening by the rebate method.
Below: This is a typical bulwark stay of the bulb plate section, but there are other forms. On a model they can be made from very narrow strips of paper.

11A The bow bulwark continues the natural curve of the rolled plate (soft nose) stem then for a few feet aft it follows the flare of the bow plating before changing to a more upright configuration above the edge of the deck, at which point it forms a sharp knuckle at the edge of the deck.

There is an alternative way of forming a bow bulwark. When the sheer has been cut and finished, and the deck outline marked, prepare a piece of lime or wood the same as that used for the hull at a thickness of 0.040in (1.0mm) and the same width as the hull block. Its length should be from a point well forward of the top of the bulwark at the stem to just aft of the after end of the bulwark. Mark the outline of the deck on the lime or wood. Cut away the middle part of the piece to within about ⅛in (3mm) of the marked deck line (see Fig 2, top). Glue and clamp it firmly in place. This is one occasion when it is useful to see glue being squeezed out from below the piece being clamped, indicating that the adhesive reaches along the deck line below. After the hull has been shaped, including the bulwark, the inside surplus wood can be pared away to leave a thin bulwark.

Bulwarks on the superstructure As superstructure bulwarks rarely require sanding they can be made from paper. For bulwarks that are positioned along the side or ends of open decks a strip of paper can be glued to the edge of a deck card. Fitting a bulwark to a navigating bridge can be less easy. If the bulwark goes round the end of the bridge wings and back inboard along the after side of the wing, the following method has proven to be the most successful. Cut a strip of paper a little wider than the height of the bulwark and draw a pencil line along it to indicate the position of the deck below the top. Glue the strip to the front of the navigating bridge deck card. Do not take it round the end of the wings at this stage, and ignore the surplus paper below the card. When the glue is dry, glue the paper round the wings to the required position. When dry, trim off the excess paper on the underside of the deck card with the tip of a No 11 blade.

Cable lifter

The cable lifter can be made in three pieces, as shown in the photograph (see Photo 12, p16): a shallow rectangular base of card, the head, and a disc of smaller diameter than the head round which the anchor cable passes, with the free end going to the spurling pipe (see Fig 3). The head is a thick turned disc with a slightly domed top.

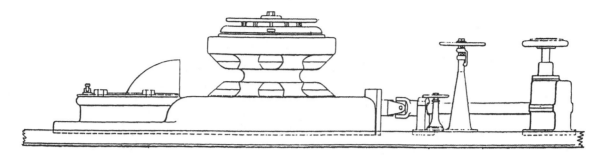

Figure 3 This is the typical form of a cable lifter. The anchor cable comes from the hawse pipe opening in the deck, round the indented part and back to (and in to) the spurling pipe.

Capstan

A mooring capstan (see Fig 4) can be made by placing a piece of round section wood in a pin vice and turning to shape the end using needle files. Usually the capstan is deck-mounted as shown (see Photo 12), although it can be set on a rectangular base about 12–18in (0.30–0.45m) deep, slightly wider than the diameter and about twice its length.

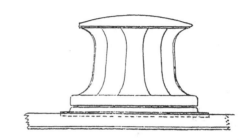

Figure 4 Elevation of a mooring capstan

11B In contrast to the previous shot this shows a bulwark that continues the natural curve or run of the flare of the bow plating. Note the bulwark stays and the bulb-angle capping rail. The windlass is electrically powered. Note the anchor stowed in a recess or pocket.

12 A pair of anchor cable lifters with a mooring capstan in the foreground.

Companionway

This steel shelter fitted on deck over a ladder or stair provides access to the deck below and can usually be made as a solid block. The width is 3ft (0.9m) or more depending on the size and number of stairs but length and height need to be confirmed from the plan. It is normally fitted with doors and the top is curved from the entrance down to the deck.

Cranes, cargo-handling

Because there are so many different types of shipboard-mounted cargo-handling cranes, this is one of those situations where a modeller has to work out the best form of construction. The accompanying photographs show two typical examples of such cranes (see Photo 13, below, and Photo 16, p23).

13 The basic elements of a cargo-handling electric crane are shown here (a further crane type can be seen in the Stulcken derrick photograph in the section on Derricks – photo 16, p23).

14A Radial davit handling a clinker-type lifeboat (note the chocks under the boat). This davit passes through the deck to a heel socket on the deck below,

Curtain plate

A narrow steel plate, on average about 12in (0.30m) wide, the curtain plate is fitted vertically along the edge of over-hanging decks. Rather than attempt to fit a narrow strip of paper to the edge of a deck card, it is better to make the deck card to the thickness of the curtain plate (see Photo 14E in Davits, p21).

Davits

Over the years a number of different methods have been designed to handle and launch a ship's lifeboats, many of which did not find much support. The main types in use are shown in photographs 14A–E in the following pages. Further examples can be seen on the vessels shown in the General Scenes photographs (pp8–10).

The radial davit can be made of fine wire bent to shape (see Fig 5, p18). If a number of davits need to be fitted it is essential that the curved part is identical on each one. A pair of pliers, with one round tapering jaw and the other concave or hollow to match, prove a useful tool for this. Radial davits

were fitted in a number of ways: they could be mounted in a pedestal casting about 3ft (0.9m) high secured to the deck, passed through the deck to a heel casting on the deck below, or placed outside the curtain plate and extended down to a heel casting fitted on the curtain plate of the deck below. The pedestal can be represented by a couple of extra coats of paint on the lower end of the davit. Boats were normally stowed on wooden chocks on deck under these davits, but occasionally they were stowed on two cast-iron pedestals, one placed a quarter of the boat's length from each end, with the keel level with the top of the adjacent guardrail.

Quadrant-type davits are made of fine wire in two parts, the rectangular frame and the davit arm with the quadrant at the lower end, and the top turned over at right angles to the plane of the quadrant. It is attached to the frame with a spot of glue, the arm being set at the correct angle. The crescent davit is made of thin wire bent to shape and secured to the deck. The 'Lum' davit is made in two parts of fine wire, the frame and the shaped arm, glued together and then to the deck (see Fig 5). The boat is stowed on chocks.

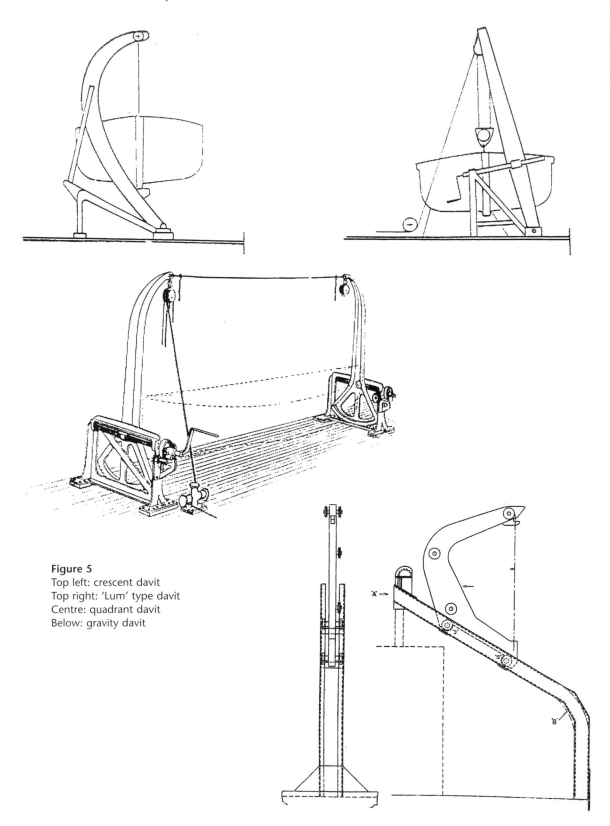

Figure 5
Top left: crescent davit
Top right: 'Lum' type davit
Centre: quadrant davit
Below: gravity davit

14B Quadrant davits.

14C Crescent davits.

The gravity davit comprises the cradle to which the boat is secured and the track down which the cradle moves. In practice the track is made up of two inward-facing steel channels with the cradle in between. At this scale it is easier to make the track as a solid piece and glue the cradle to it. The track can be made of wire, and again it is essential to make sure that all track pieces are identical. In most cases the inboard end of the track rests on an adjacent deckhouse. An alternative method of making the trackway is to use 0.010in (0.25mm) thick card. Cut a strip with a width equal to the total length of the track from deck edge to inboard end plus the length (height) of any support to a deckhouse top. Draw

14D A typical gravity davit arrangement.

14E Two other types of davit can be seen in this photograph.

a pencil line along the strip parallel to one edge and in from the edge by the distance from the edge of the deck to the point where the sloping part of the track turns down to become vertical. Draw a similar line down the other side, the distance in from the edge by the length of the vertical support on the deckhouse to the inboard end of the sloping part of the trackway. With a blunt tool score a shallow indent along the two pencil lines, taking care not to cut right through the card. Cut off narrow strips 2ft (0.60m) wide to scale from one end of the card and bend at the score mark to the required shape, keeping the score on the inside of the bend. They can be glued in place on the model at an appropriate time during construction. When creating the cradles it is easier to form these of fine wire without the lower part that rests on the track and to secure them in place after the boat has been glued to the trackways, using the inboard side of the boat to support the wire. This provides a better opportunity to adjust each cradle piece for height and alignment. To make sure that all the boats sit on the trackways at the same height,(around 8ft or 2.4m to scale) above the deck, a distance piece must be put under each while the glue is drying. When there is no deckhouse to support the inboard end of a trackway this is done by means of

an 'A'-frame support. The boat winches associated with these davits can be created using blocks of wood to scale 2ft (0.60m) square and 4ft (1.22m) high.

Deck cards

If a deck extends beyond the side or end of a deckhouse the whole house should be covered with a piece of thin card to form the extension. Where appropriate, the thickness of the card will equal that of a curtain plate.

Deckhouses

Stripwood of appropriate thickness can be used to make the deckhouses, the shape of which should be taken from the plan. When a long house is not the same width along its whole length, it is easier to make it in several pieces to suit the different widths. If the deck card does not cover the butts, the top should be covered with paper trimmed to the shape of the house. Whenever a house is covered with a deck card the correct deck height can be maintained by reducing the thickness of the house by that of the card. It is essential to maintain correct deck height at all times; failure to do so will adversely affect the overall appearance and character of the ship.

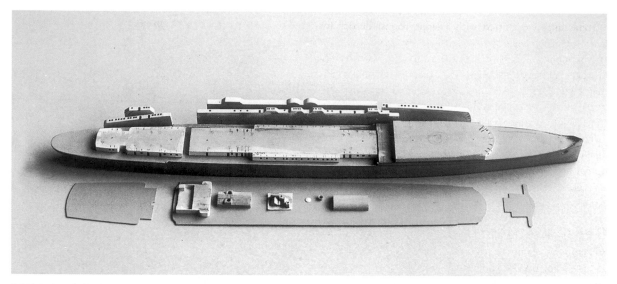

15 This shows the hull of the Cunard liner *Lusitania* with a few deckhouses in place, with further deckhouses and deck cards alongside ready to be fitted. The two items at bottom centre are small deck units that were assembled after the holes for ventilators had been drilled in larger pieces of wood, which were then cut down to the appropriate size and assembled on a paper base.

Deck stanchions

Stanchions run along the outboard side of open decks as vertical supports for the deck above. They can vary in width between 6in and 24in (0.12m and 0.60m). The distance between them varies according to their size: the narrow ones are closely spaced, about 5–6ft (1.52–1.82m), with the spacing increasing at the same rate as the stanchions, as can be seen by looking at the plans. Small stanchions can be made from very fine wire or plastic rod, with stiff paper or thin card suitable for larger ones. A spot of glue at each end will secure them in position. It is essential that they are correctly spaced as on the plan and absolutely vertical, unless shown set at an angle. There is a simple way to produce the very small stanchions fitted between the top of a bulwark and the deck above. Having made the bulwark and checked that it fits in place, lay it flat so the inside is uppermost, and mark on it the positions of the stanchions. Glue short lengths of the stanchion material across the bulwark at these positions, keeping them upright. At this stage their length is unimportant, but the lower end must be kept to the depth of the rebate above the bottom of the bulwark piece (see Fig 6). When dry, place the piece on a hard surface and press down firmly with a block of wood to ensure that the stanchions are in firm contact with the bulwark. With a sharp blade trim the stanchions to length and secure the bulwark in place on the hull. Check once more for correct alignment and then secure the stanchion by applying, with the point of a very fine paintbrush, a touch of clear matt varnish to the top.

Figure 6 The diagram shows the method of fitting deck stanchions to a bulwark in way of an opening in a hull, or to one along an open promenade deck with another deck above. Random lengths of the stanchion material are glued to the inside of the bulwark, with the lower end level with the bottom of the bulwark if being fitted on the edge of the deck, or above this if being fitted by the rebate method. When dry the stanchions can be trimmed to length and the item fitted. A touch of clear matt varnish will secure the tops of the stanchions.

Derricks

Derricks are also known as booms. Originally of wood, cargo derricks now are of tubular steel construction, though occasionally derricks built from steel angles or channels with flat bar lattice-style bracing were fitted on some early vessels. Their length must be taken from the plan. Derricks can be made from entomological pins with the head removed, or from fine wire that has been straightened by rolling on a hard surface. Material with a diameter of 12in (0.30m) will be suitable for most vessels. The derricks can be attached to the post or mast by turning 1mm of one end at right angles and fixing it in place with a touch of Instant Glue. If the derricks are being shown in the working position, then the angle will have to be less.

Some ships were fitted with a large, robust derrick for heavy lifts. Such derricks were usually stowed upright on the after side of the foremast, with the lower end of the derrick in a heel casting on the deck. Two or more massive, multi-sheave blocks with wires, well shrouded in canvas for weather protection, were positioned at the top of the derrick, which can be represented by small blobs of glue worked into a suitable shape and then painted. Later, as the need for much greater lifting capacity grew, so new and more sophisticated heavy-lifting equipment came to be fitted on general cargo ships. One such, widely adopted, was the Stulcken derrick.

Derrick posts

Sometimes called Samson Posts, derrick posts were on average 24–30in (0.60–0.75m) in diameter and were generally fitted with a top (see Fig 7). Cross-bracing in the form of a solid or latticework structure is fitted between a pair of posts placed just below the gap. The posts can be made from pins of appropriate diameter, with the heads filed to the shape shown. Where a ventilation head is situated (as in Fig 7) the original head will have to be removed and replaced by one of the correct shape, which can be made by turning the end of a cocktail stick to the shape indicated. The derricks are attached to the post by heel fittings generally some 7ft (2.14m) above the deck. Examples of derrick posts can be seen in the photograph of *Aragon* (see Photo 11A, p14).

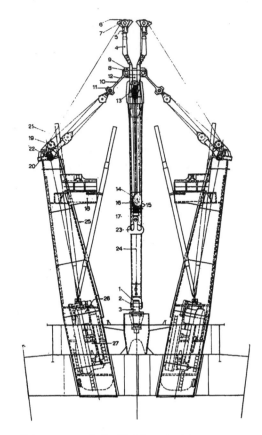

Figure 7 Arrangement of a Stulcken derrick

16 At the centre of this photograph a Stulcken derrick installation is shown.

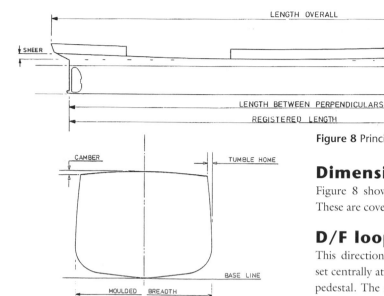

Figure 8 Principal hull dimensions

Dimensions

Figure 8 shows the principle dimensions of a ship's hull. These are covered in detail in the section on Hulls (see p29).

D/F loop

This direction-finding appliance comprises two wire rings set centrally at right angles to each other and mounted on a pedestal. The rings are about 3ft (0.90m) in diameter, and should be made of very thin wire. They are usually found on the top of the wheelhouse (see Davits, Photo 14E, p21).

Doors

Wooden doors can be represented by rectangles of brown-painted cigarette paper 0.060in x 0.025in. They can either be glued in place or secured with a touch of clear matt var nish. When fixing, the bottom of the door must be kept 12in (0.30m) scale height above the deck, this distance being the average height of a door sill.

Fairleads

The most frequently encountered type of fairlead is that shown in the diagram (see Fig 9, top). Other types may have one, two or three rollers, the diameters of which range from

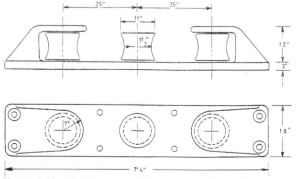

Figure 9 This shows a typical three-roller fairlead. The dimensions are suitable for a medium-size vessel. Two- and four-roller versions are frequently used and dimensions vary according to size of ship and position of the fairleads.

17 A typical fiddley grating: the size (area) depends on that of the vessel and its boiler room requirements.

18B This is a typical arrangement of siren and maintenance platform on a funnel. This form of siren is operated by compressed air. Note the blackening of the paintwork by the exhaust gases showing that this was a diesel engine ship.

about 6–12in (0.15–0.30m) according to the size of the vessel (see Fig 9, bottom). Fairleads are fitted to the deck, as close as possible to the edge, but some are mounted on steel seats or stools.

Fiddley gratings

These steel gratings fitted on the boiler casing adjacent to a funnel comprise an angle bar frame and a number of closely spaced steel bars. They vary in size and shape according to the vessel on which they are fitted. On a model they can be represented by pieces of black-painted thin card cut to the required shape(s) and glued in place.

Funnels

For many years funnels were either round or oval in section, and whilst some other shapes appeared before the last war, it was only in the post-war years that the variety of shape and size in funnels became more widespread. From the modelling aspect each kind of funnel requires its own method.

Round funnels can be made from thin-wall plastic or metal tube, with the bottom cut at an angle to give the cor-

rect rake. Oval funnels can be made from thin-wall metal tube of a diameter which, when the tube is gently squeezed, will have the correct length, width and oval shape required. Where no material of suitable diameter is available, then the following method will produce an oval funnel and, if required, a round funnel. Prepare a wood mandrel a few inches long, so that its cross-section is slightly less than the overall cross-section of the funnel. It must be well waxed to prevent glue adhering to it later. Wind a strip of thin paper several times round the mandrel, gluing the paper to itself as it is wound round. It is better to make the free end of the paper strip finish at the point where a waste steam pipe will be fitted later. When dry, this cut edge can be gently sanded smooth and the tube removed from the mandrel. Once a piece of the right length has been cut off, the bottom must be trimmed to give the right rake. The funnel can be secured in place by inserting a pin in the deck at the centre of the funnel's position, leaving about ¼in (5mm) projecting above the deck. When the time comes to fit the funnel, fill the lower half with glue and place it in position over the pin, adjusting for rake and transverse verticality.

18A Carving an irregularly shaped funnel from the solid.

On some ships the funnel is fitted with a cowl top as can be seen in the photograph of The Allan Line's *Calgarian* (see Photo 9C, p9). As the edge is heavily beveled the shape or outline of the cowl in plan view, top and bottom, should be marked out on a piece of thin wood about 0.020in thick and considerably larger than the area of the finished cowl. Leaving plenty of excess wood outside the oval to reduce the chance of the wood splitting, drill a small hole in the center of the oval. Cut away the surplus wood almost to the outline of the base of the cowl and then glue the funnel in the accurate position. When the glue has set sand the cowl to shape, including the bevelled edge.

Funnels should not be painted until the whistle and its platform have been fitted. The waste steam pipes, made of very thin wire secured in a hole in the deck very close to the funnel, can be added once a funnel is in place. On motor ships the funnel is usually plated over a few feet below the top and pierced by a number of exhaust pipes of different diameters. The way to make such a funnel is to carve it to shape and cut to the height of the plated top, remembering to form the bottom to the correct rake. Two or three turns of thin paper should be wrapped and glued round the funnel, keeping the top edge the right height above the top of the wood block. The exhaust outlets can be represented by inserting short lengths of pins, with the exposed end filed flat, into holes drilled in the top of the block.

Glass cases

A completed model should always be placed in a dust-proof case; in fact it should be kept in a similar working case or cover whenever possible throughout construction. There are several methods of making such a case, and that described here has been found satisfactory. In settling on the overall dimensions, these must relate to those of the model: if there is too little space between model and glass it will look cramped; too much and it will look lost.

The base is made up of the baseboard on which is fastened a plinth of the same wood, with the moulded edge piece outside, leaving a channel for the glass (see Fig 10). These pieces should be finished by polishing, varnishing or another method to suit the modeller's preference. Four small feet should be glued to the underside of the baseboard. The model on its base is secured to the plinth by wood screws put in from the underside of the baseboard in holes drilled through both baseboard and plinth. It is advisable to prepare these items at an early stage, drilling the holes and marking their positions on the wood that will be used for the model's baseboard and put in pilot holes at these points. The glass must not be a tight fit against the wood forming the channel in which it sits. The bottom of the channel is lined with plasticine, into which the glass cover is firmly pressed. Plasticine is also used to fill the gap outside between glass and edge moulding.

The glass should be as thin as possible for the size of case. The edges can be joined with passe-partout strip or gummed brown-paper strip. This can be covered on the outside with thin strips of veneer to match the baseboard. A small plate should be fixed to the case, either externally or internally, giving the name of the ship, date of build, owner and scale. It is helpful to put a label on the underside of the case containing further details of the ship, name and address of the modeller and date when model was built.

It may seem too obvious to mention here, but a case must

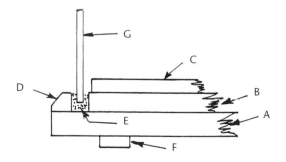

Figure 10
A cross-section through the bottom of a case, showing: base (A); plinth (B); baseboard of model (C); edge moulding (D); plasticine bed for glass (E); one of the four feet (F).

19 On the glass case shown here the edges were secured with *passe-partout*, a strong adhesive tape.

always be lifted by its base, never by holding the glass cover.

Guard rails

Even if rails can be made absolutely to the exact scale sizes, it is not really practical to attempt to fit them to a 1/1200-scale model. Consider these impossible sizes: the ball-type stanchions, which taper slightly from a diameter of around 1¾in to 1½in or less (0.0014in to 0.0012in or 0.036mm to 0.030mm in scale); the bars or rails average ¾in (0.0006in or 0.015mm in scale) in diameter and the ball through which they pass, forged with the stanchion, is about twice the diameter of the tail; the height is usually 3ft 6in to 3ft 9in (0.035in in scale) to the top of the rail or underside of the wood capping rail where fitted.

Hatches

The coamings of cargo hatches on weather decks are about 3ft (0.92m) high. The cross (transverse) coamings are peaked about 9in (0.22m) at the centre. This gives a slight downward slope to the hatch covers from the centre line outwards. As this is so slight at 1/1200 scale, hatches can be made from flat rectangles of wood. Tarpaulins were used to cover the hatches and the colour of the tarpaulin could be black, green, grey or natural canvas depending on the practices of the ship owner.

Hatches that were fitted with mechanically operated steel covers were of a slightly greater overall height with a flat top (i.e. the cross coamings were not peaked). These slab covers were about 12in (0.30m) deep, and extended slightly beyond the side coamings. They will have to be made of two pieces, one a scale 3ft (0.91m) thick to the size of the hatch coamings, with a second piece about a scale 12in (0.30m) thick and a scale 12in wider each side, which will be glued on top. To uncover the hatch the separate covers were pulled to one end, where they automatically rotated through 90 degrees to stow vertically on the deck. The side coamings were extended the length of the stowage area to enable this to be done.

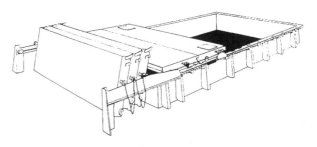

Figure 11 Method of stowing sliding hatch covers

20A The coaming of a cargo hatch fitted with wood board covers, over which tarpaulins are secured.

20B A cargo hatch fitted with sliding steel (slab) covers. No tarpaulins are required with such covers.

Hulls

The hull is most important part of a model: unless the sheer and the shape of bow and stern are absolutely correct, the character of the vessel will be lost. There are several basic hull forms: flush deck, flush deck with forecastle, flush deck with forecastle and poop, and the three island type with forecastle, bridge and poop.

There are some key dimensions applied to a hull. Length overall (LOA) is the greatest length of the hull from the fore side of the top of the stem to the aftermost part of the stern. Length between perpendiculars (LBP) is the length between the forward perpendicular (FP) and the after perpendicular (AP). The FP is a perpendicular to the base line passing through the point of intersection of the stem and the summer load line. The AP is a similar line on the after face of the stern frame. Where there is no stern frame, the AP is the centre of the rudder stock. Moulded (Mld) breadth is the maximum breadth of the hull amidships to the outside of the frame. Draught is the distance between the waterline and the underside of the keel.

Although there are a number of ways of producing a hull for a miniature model, the most satisfactory one for those ships covered here (and all similar vessels) is to carve it in solid wood, preferably English lime. Much of the lime currently available in model shops is basswood, which although has characteristics akin to those of English lime and carves quite well also tends to fray, and there is some difficulty at times in obtaining a really sharp edge. The first step when making a hull is to prepare a block of wood with overall dimensions slightly greater than those of the hull. A centre line must be marked along the top and bottom of the block, taking care to ensure that they are in line vertically. Three

21A This is a good example of a bar stem, with a short spirket plate at the top above deck level. This can be made in two pieces and then glued to the deck edge. Note the short strengthening plate at the break of the forecastle.

21B This gives a very clear indication of the shape of a counter stern (although the dark underwater section is only of value for a full hull model).

templates need to be made, using good-quality thin card. The first is the sheer template, which is made to the line of the deck to which the hull block will be carved. If the finished model is to be mounted on a painted board (see Seas, p38) the bottom of the template should be to a line 2ft (0.60m) to scale below the load waterline, but if the model is to be set in a moulded sea then the block will have to be made deeper to match the thickness of the moulded sea. This will allow a narrow line of the boot topping to be included on the hull. The outline of the stem and stern should be included. The second template is for the outline of the deck to which the sheer is being cut, which can be taken from the plan, as can that of the third template, which

is of the load waterline. These can be combined in one template if preferred (see Fig 12). It is best to use the FP and AP as the key lines, which should be marked on the templates and on the top, bottom and both sides of the block. The outline of each template should be marked on the block using a chisel-pointed medium soft pencil.

The sheer is the first to be carved, using a very sharp chisel. To avoid a shaving 'running' due to an adverse change in grain, it is useful to make a series of saw cuts across the block with a fine tenon saw, stopping just above the line of the sheer. When most of the wood has been removed, pare away the wood along each side over a width of about ⅛in at a slight angle down to the sheer line (see Fig 12). This acts as

Figure 12
Above: the sheer hull template; the rectangular extension below the waterline is to provide a means of holding it.
Below: the top half is the outline of the deck on which the sheer has been cut; the other half is the shape of the waterline, which will be marked on the underside of the hull block. The template is turned over for the other half to be marked.

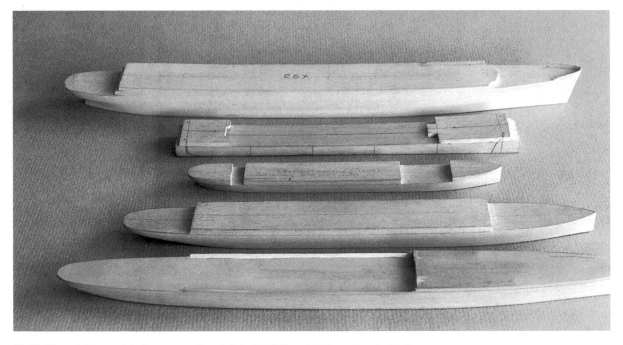

21C Different forms of hull construction (all to 1/1200 scale), from top to bottom:
The top hull, of the Italian liner *Rex*, was carved to include the lowest superstructure deck and the bow bulwark integrally with the main block, and cut away at the stern to the level of the lowest open deck.
On the second example (Silver Line's *Silverbriar*) the sheer has been cut, the profile shape of bow and stern marked on each side, and pieces for the forecastle and poop fitted. Note that the inboard ends of these have been cut to the true shape before being fixed to the hull block.
On this hull (Cunard liner *Carmania*) the sheer was cut to the line of the top of the midship house, and then cut down to the level of the next lower deck at each end.
As there was only a short well deck forward and aft on the next ship (Bibby Line's *Leicestershire*), the sheer was cut to the line of the poop, bridge and forecastle, after which the two wells were cut.
On the final model (Cunard liner *Lusitania*) the sheer was cut to three levels. First the whole block was cut to the line of the forecastle deck. Then from a point abaft midships to the stern it was cut to the line of the top of the bulwark on the next deck down. Lastly, it was cut to the level of that deck from the after end of the bulwark to the stern. After that the hull was carved to shape. A cut was made each side 2mm inside the edge of the hull for the length of the bulwark, and the wood between the cuts removed to deck level. Finally, the 2mm thickness of the bulwark was reduced to little more than paper thickness.

a visible guide to the deck edge at sheer-line level, and reduces the chance of accidentally cutting below the marked line at the edge. Then remove the remainder of the wood rest down to the sheer line marked on each side of the block When the surface has been sanded smooth, re-mark the lines showing the position of the FP and AP, the centre line, followed by the outline of the deck from the template. On the underside mark the outline of the waterline from the template.

Before starting to shape the sides of the hull cut the ends to the profile of the stem and stern. In the case of the stem finish the cut just clear of the pencil line to allow for final trimming to it after the work on the sides has been completed. On each side remove the wood with vertical cuts to just outside the pencil line of the deck. The body-plan, or the cross-sections, shows the amount of flare at the fore end and the shape of the sides aft. Modellers will develop their

own way of carving the hollow flare on each side of the bow, working from deck to waterline and starting each cut just below the deck edge. Gouges and files are not really satisfactory tools for this; the Swann Morton Surgical Blades Nos 10, 11, 15 and 23 are much better at paring away the wood. When the flare has been formed, sand away to the deck-edge pencil line to leave a very narrow flat edge to the deck, which needs to be sanded down. To limit damage to the deck edge during sanding the block should be held with the ball of the thumb on the deck and slightly over the edge. Use very fine or worn sandpaper tightly rolled in a fore and aft direction up against the thumb. Finally trim and sand the stem to its line and shape.

For a cruiser stern, with its convex sides, a straight blade such as a Swann Morton No 11 can be used to pare away the surplus wood to the right shape, finally sanding away to the pencil line of the deck edge and waterline. Again, the

21D This shows the shape of a typical cruiser stern, which in this instance is somewhat full-bodied.

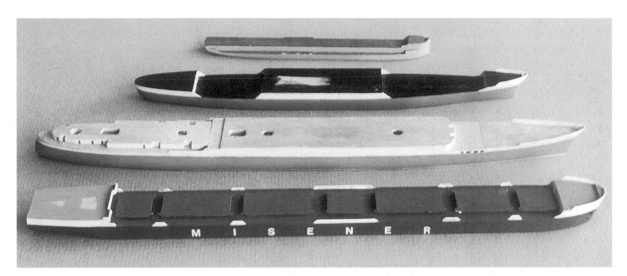

21E Hulls at a more advanced stage and ready for the addition of the superstructure, from top to bottom:
This is the finished hull for a trunk deck steamer (Ropner's *Clearpool*) and should not to be confused with the turret-type design of hull. The bulwark pieces, with freeing ports cut out, have been added and the forecastle with stem spirket plate fitted.

This is a typical poop, bridge and forecastle hull, with rolled plate stem and bow bulwark fitted. The unpainted area is to provide a key for the glue when the deckhouse is fitted. The paint will be removed in way of hatches, etc, before they are fitted.

The Union Castle Line's *Pendennis Castle* is ready for the superstructure to be added. Note that the sides are finished on the house in way of an open deck aft, with the doors and windows in place, and bollards have been fitted on deck. Such work has to be done before a deck card is put in place. The two rectangular openings are for the swimming pools.

The large bulk carrier hull is complete with all hatches fitted, and ready to have the combined bridge/accommodation block, built as a separate unit, installed, and the forecastle gear added. The vessel is a sister ship to the *Saskatchewan Pioneer* illustrated elsewhere, but her hull is deep blue with white upperworks.

21F The partly completely model of the *Beavercove*: its working baseboard has been secured to a thick block of wood for stability, and to enable the model to be turned on its side when the work demands.

body plan or cross sections will indicate the shape. A counter stern is more difficult to form. The photograph on page 30 shows clearly the general shape and characteristics. When carving it is essential to form the knuckle lines with a sharp edge. The profile of the stern formed earlier shows their position and also the angle of the counter plating. Both of these, it will be seen, gradually blend into the side plating, the angle of the counter plating decreasing as it curves round to become more vertical.

When the hull is finished it should be mounted on a working baseboard, approximately 2in (5cm) longer than the model, ¾in (or about 2cm) wider each side, and ¼in (5mm) thick. The model should be placed centrally on the board and secured with two fine wood screws from below on the centre line. When it comes to painting the hull, a thin distance piece slightly narrower and shorter than the hull should be inserted between the board and the hull. Without it there is a danger of a fillet of paint forming along the bottom edge of the hull and the board. If this working baseboard is then secured to a block of wood 2in (5cm) square and longer than the baseboard, it provides a firm support when working on the model, and it will not tip over if placed on its side (see the *Beavercove*, Photo 21F, p33).

Jackstaff

This short vertical pole or staff set vertically on the centre line just abaft the stem can be made from a short length of very fine wire.

Lifeboats

Until comparatively recently stowed lifeboats were fitted with covers, usually of canvas. Such boats can be made in the following way. A strip of wood several inches long should be prepared, the width being the scale breadth of the lifeboat and the thickness the scale depth of the boat from its bottom to top of stem. A centre line should be marked along the top of the wood and a bevel filed on each side of the centre line to produce a cross-section (see Fig 13). Mark the length of a boat from one end, cut off the corner of the free end on each side of the centre line at an angle and sand off to the shape of the bow. Cut off the boat and repeat the process at the other end. In plan view wooden lifeboats had much more shape to the sides and a finer pointed bow than

those built later of metal. The latter had bluff ends and quite a length of parallel body amidships.

Lifeboats were generally stowed singly under their handling davits, but sometimes they were nested, which means that a slightly smaller boat was stowed on top of and partially within a larger one. Alternatively, a second boat of the same size was stowed on bearers above the first with a clear gap between the two. Some ships also carried collapsible boats, which were stowed on deck under a lifeboat. These can be represented on a miniature model by a flat piece of wood, the same length and breadth as the boat under which it is stowed, and 2ft deep in scale, with similar though more bluff ends, and the bottom corners slightly rounded. Occasionally they were stowed elsewhere on deck either singly or in stacks of two or three.

Masts

Masts can be made either from entomological pins (after removal of head as they are used pointed end upwards) or sewing needles. Signal yards and gaffs are made from fine wire, and the crow's nest from a minute scrap of wood. To allow for final adjustments to rake and verticality make the hole into which a mast will be inserted slightly oversize. A spot of glue in the hole will fix it in place, Instant Glue (see p11) being the best. Outriggers, when fitted, can be cut from wood and glued on each side of the mast. As these are flat on top but angled on the underside it is essential to ensure that the two pieces are identical. The thickness is the same as the diameter of the mast at that point. They vary in shape and size, and the diagram shows a typical example (see Fig 14).

Materials

Wood English lime and basswood have been suggested for hulls. Other softwoods can be used, provided they will hold an edge, do not have a pronounced grain, are free from knots and will give a smooth finish. Basswood is available in model shops (see Appendix II, pp205–206) in a wide range of widths of different thickness, and square, rectangular and round in cross section. It is useful for deckhouses and for many of the fittings. If a standard thickness is fractionally less than that required for a deckhouse, the difference can be made up with thin card glued to the underside.

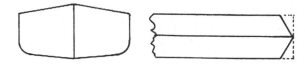 

Figure 13 The sequence for making lifeboats

Figure 14
A typical form of the derrick outrigger, although size, shape and form can vary.

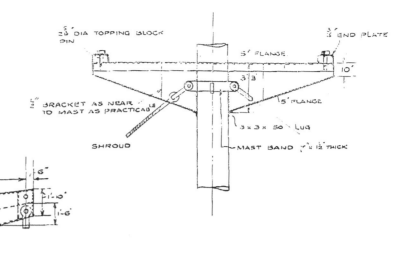

22 An example of a simple derrick table on a mast, using two large cowl ventilators as end supports. Note the pair of handed electric winches and the deep curtain plate to the overhanging deck.

Card A number of pieces of different thickness are required, preferably Bristol board, or similar, with a smooth surface.

Abrasive papers ('sandpaper') Garnet paper and the different oxide types offer the modeller greater range and control than the grades of paper generally available in DIY shops, although these can be useful. A very handy gadget for use in sanding operations is a sanding stick, which is a piece of wood about 6in long and ½in square. A strip of sandpaper can be fixed on each of the four sides over about half its length. As there are four sides, four different grades of paper can be used. It is useful to keep a stick with well-worn paper on it.

Pins Entomological pins, both with and without heads, have many uses on these models, as do ordinary dressmaking, household and stationery or office pins. However, avoid steel pins, for they can damage the fine sharp edge of some end cutting pliers.

Needles Sewing needles are useful for making masts, as they have more taper over their length than long pins

Wire This can be obtained from many sources both commercial and from old electrical equipment (see Appendix II, pp205–206). Soft brass and copper wire are best, but fuse wire has many uses as does electric cable and flex. Stripped of insulation, these can provide strands of wire in a good range of diameters (the micrometer is most necessary here).

Mounted shavings

These shavings of softwood glued to very thin paper prevent the wood from splitting when being used. The shavings should be taken from a block of wood at least 1in wide, using a plane with the blade set to give a fine cut. The plane blade must be honed to extreme sharpness. The shavings will probably come off curled up. They can be straightened by lightly dampening them as they are unrolled, after which they should be glued on to very thin paper and placed under, and kept under, a heavy weight.

Navigation lights

The port (red) and starboard (green) navigation lights (lamps) were fitted on the outboard end of the navigation bridge or a similar adjacent locality. Each set comprised two lamps, a stand-by oil lamp above an electric lamp. They were mounted at the after end of a backboard about 3ft (0.90m) long. Board and outside of the lamps are painted red or

green. However, at some time in the 1960s or thereabouts the outside of the lamps and the boards were painted matt black. Lamps can be represented with a spot of glue.

Paints, brushes, painting

Only paints specially prepared for modelmakers, which provide good covering power from a very thin coat, should be considered for these models. One such, widely available, is Humbrol. There is a good range of colours, in gloss, semi-matt and matt finish, though not all colours are to be found in all three finishes. Similar paints are available from other manufacturers: model shops may be able to supply details. Although there is a wide range of colours, these may not include the particular one used by a specific company – the lavender shade on the Union Castle Line's hulls is a case in point. In such circumstances the shade has to be obtained by mixing.

Brushes The best brushes are artist's sable hair, although there are several other types of bristle or combinations of bristle, including synthetic bristles, available from a number of manufacturers of artists' materials. The most useful sizes to obtain are: round 0000, 000, 00, 0,1 and 2; flats, also called one-stroke or shaders, ⅛in, ¼in, and ⅜in, (metric sizes available are 3, 6, 9, 10, 12mm). Brushes must be thoroughly cleaned after use, and always stored bristle end up. If possible brushes used for white paint should not be used for other colours. Whenever practical, items should be painted before being fitted, always keeping in mind that on very small objects their size can be materially altered by a couple of coats of paint.

Painting When painting these miniature models even a thin coat of paint can detrimentally alter the size of some fittings and thus make them appear oversize. This is most noticeable on items such as davits, masts and derricks. Alternatively, there are occasions when paint, in the form of some extra coats, can be used to bring something up to the required size. A good example is to apply several coats to the bottom 3ft (0.90m) of a pedestal-mounted radial davit to represent the pedestal.

Plans

Plans available to the ship modeller fall into several categories. Shipbuilders' plans, such as have survived, come in three forms. The design drawings show the client the appearance and layout of the proposed vessel, but they lack much in the way of weather deck details. If nothing else is available, they can, when used in conjunction with photo-

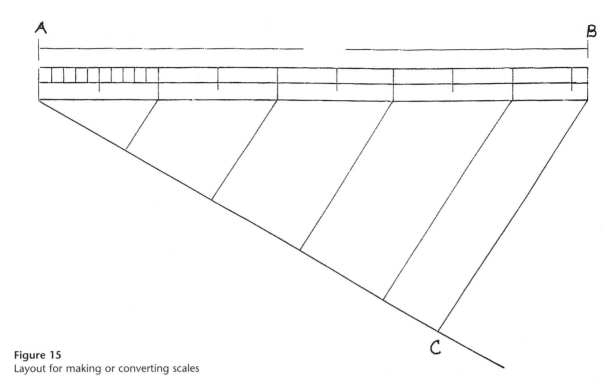

Figure 15
Layout for making or converting scales

graphs to check for external changes, provide the basis for a model. General-arrangement (GA) drawings are generally well detailed, and comprise external profile, rigging plan, sometimes a sectional elevation, and general arrangements of all decks. They usually contain a useful amount of deck detail. 'As fitted' drawings show the ship as completed and are in essence up-dated versions of the general-arrangement plans. The lines plan comprises a sheer or side elevation of the hull showing the position of the waterlines, buttock lines, FP and AP and station lines. Below this is the half-breadth plan showing the shape of the water line and deck line. To one side is the body plan showing half cross sections of the hull at the station lines along its length.

The technical journals are a useful source of plans for a wide variety of vessels, though the amount of detail shown does vary. Information about vessels for which all shipyard data was destroyed can sometimes be found here. Plans specifically for modelmakers are available from various commercial sources (see Appendix II, pp205–206). Some may include constructional details, while others are well-detailed arrangement drawings.

Portholes

Sometimes called sidelights, these can vary in size between 10in (0.25m) and 18in (0.45m) in diameter, depending on position on hull or deckhouse. Those in skylights were

smaller. Once their positions have been marked it is advisable to make a small, shallow indent with the blunted point of a pin. A spot of black ink should then be applied to each with a tubular drawing pen, selecting a size of pen that will give the required diameter of the porthole.

Rigging

As with the matter of adding guard rails and rigging to a 1/1200-scale model, the sizes of rope and wire necessary for rigging are just too small to make this job worthwhile.

Scales, making or converting

Method: along the long edge of a sheet of paper draw two lines parallel to the edge, one 5mm and the other 12mm from the edge. At A on the lower line erect a perpendicular up to the edge of the sheet. On the lower line from A mark the length BP of the vessel as measured from the original plan. Call this length AB, and erect a perpendicular at B. Assume that the measured length AB is 8.45in and that the length BP of the ship is 580ft, or 5.8in at 1/1200 scale. From A draw a line at no more than 30 degrees to AB. From A mark a length AC on this line of 5.8in. Mark the 1in units from A along the line. Draw a line from C to B. Draw lines parallel to CB from the 1in points on AC to the lower of the two lines along the top. At each of the intersection points on AB erect perpendiculars to the edge of the paper. The distance between each of these perpendiculars is equal to 100ft except for the last one, which is 80ft. These can be subdivided as required. If the BP length on the plan is too long for the sheet of paper being used, then take a suitable proportion of it, say, a quarter or a half, and make this the length AB. Similarly, mark the same proportion of the length BP of the ship as AC.

Seas

Rather than mount a completed model on a plain wood baseboard, its appearance can be enhanced if it is set in a sea of some kind. This can be done in various ways. The simplest is just a painted board, in the nondescript, muddy, grey-green colour of an estuary. In such a setting it would be appropriate to show the ship lying with one anchor down – indicated by a length of anchor cable running from one hawse hole to a point ahead of the ship. Alternatively, paint the boards a blue-green, and add the wash and wake with white paint applied while the main colour is still wet. Aerial photographs of similar ships will give a good idea of what is required. If a moulded sea is contemplated, then wave height (scale), and wind direction must be taken into consideration. Again, reference to photographs will show wave patterns and formations. Showing flecks of white to random wave crests will add atmosphere. At all costs avoid uniformity, such as waves in lines and of uniform height and depths of troughs. The scale of the model must also be kept in mind.

The medium for sculptured seas can be plasticine, or a modelling compound or paste. Mark the shape of the waterline on the board then apply the medium, working it up to,

but not over this line. When putting the model in place, it must not come into contact with the medium. Any slight gaps between model and medium can be made good once it has been secured to the board. The sea must be painted before the model is put in place. Apart from Humbrol or a similar product, acrylic paint or artist's oil colour can be used, but avoid a glossy finish on the sea. Start with a coat of matt white over the whole area. The desired colour of the sea can be obtained by mixing together in varying proportions the three primary colours, red, blue and yellow. When satisfied with the result after the model has been added, the assembly can be put in its glass case and sealed up.

Skylights

The majority of skylights have a cross section (see Fig 16) and their size and length will vary according to their purpose. The best way to make them is to prepare a short length of wood to the cross section shown, and to cut off pieces equal to the length of the particular skylight. The hinged lids in the closed position can be represented, if so desired, by rectangles of thin paper. The portholes can be represented by dots of black ink. Where rectangular panes of glass are fitted, these can be cut from a strip of very thin

Figure 16
Cross-section through a Light & Air (L & A) skylight on the outside of a deckhouse

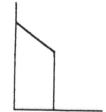

23 This is an example of a painted baseboard with the wash and wake worked up while the base colour was still wet.

black paper (blackened cigarette paper, for instance) and fixed in place.

Another form of skylight is often found on plans marked as L & A, short for Light and Air (see Fig 16); they can be formed in the same way as above. L & A skylights are usually sited along the side of a deckhouse and also across the end of small deckhouses or casings. They are usually no more than 2ft (0.60m) wide and up to 3ft (0.91m) high at the back, with a 30 degrees downward sloping top. Portholes, or rectangular panes of glass, on the sloping top provide the light source.

Superstructure front and side covering

When there are a number of rectangular windows across the front or along the side of a superstructure, they can be formed with a good degree of accuracy and uniformity as follows, but it does require access to a photocopying machine that can enlarge or reduce in single-unit steps.

On a sheet of paper no bigger than A3, draw out the shape of the vertical flush part of the front or side of the superstructure, including bulwark and any short side bulwarks joined to it, several times the finished scale size, and mark in the position of each window. Black in these rectangles. If a sharper copy is required trace this drawing on to a sheet of draughting film. Use the tracing on the photocopier to reduce the drawing to the required scale size

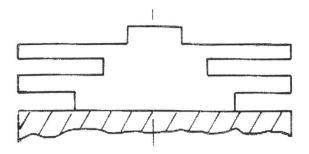

Figure 17
This is an example of an expanded paper covering for the front of a superstructure. If necessary the pieces forming the bulwarks can be increased in length to be turned round the side of the deck. The original drawing is made several times the required scale size, then reduced by photocopying.

and make a number of copies. Depending upon the enlarged size of the original drawing, this reduction may have to be done in stages.

All that remains to be done is to cut out one of the copies very carefully to the outline, and check it in place to see if everything aligns correctly. If it does not, then cut out another copy. Before cutting out a piece for the bridge front give all the copies a coat of clear matt varnish; the black on the window areas should not lift or smudge.

Swimming pools

The pool is formed by a pool-shaped hole cut in the deckhouse before it is fitted in place. After painting the sides and

24 The front and sides of this superstructure unit were covered by the photocopying method.

25 A typical pool layout of a large passenger liner

bottom of the pool once the deckhouse has been fitted, the water can be represented by a piece of clear Perspex placed in the pool, with the top surface of the Perspex just below the deck edge. The tiled pool surround is cut from a piece of very thin card.

Tools

Tools for a job are largely a matter of personal choice. These miniature models can be made with quite a modest kit of tools, such as: Swann Morton blades in a number of shapes with handle; flat, round and triangular needle files; a pair of end cutting pliers (those that give a square cut); a pair of either milliner's or long-nose pliers with side cutter; 6in steel rule with metric and imperial scales; a small square; a pin vice; Archimedean drill; two pin chucks (one that closes completely and one that closes to leave a small opening to take twist or other drill bits); two pairs of tweezers (one with pointed points and one with angled points); Swann Morton tenon saw blade; small steel hand plane; several small G-clamps. One further tool is essential: a micrometer (or Verniers calipers as an alternative). This tool is required for

determining the diameter and thickness of materials but does not need to have a very large jaw capacity, one inch being quite adequate.

Other useful tools include a 1in flat chisel for cutting the sheer, a small bench vice, a magnifying glass (or jeweller's loupe or linen tester, which are available in a range of magnifications) and a selection of dental burrs (drills) or their equivalent now available from model shops: of particular use is the one with a ball head for removing the pith from seeds, which can be used to form ventilator cowls. It is possible to purchase very small diameter drills, but these can break very easily. Quite satisfactory holes can be made using pins of different sizes with a point formed at one end, and used in a pin chuck or the Archimedean drill: brass pins will bend rather than break (thus avoiding the problem of extracting the broken tip of a drill from below the surface of the wood). A small bench vice will be found useful at times. Other tools could be mentioned, such as a mini electric drill with a selection of accessories and a bench vice with swivel head, but these are a matter of personal preference and choice.

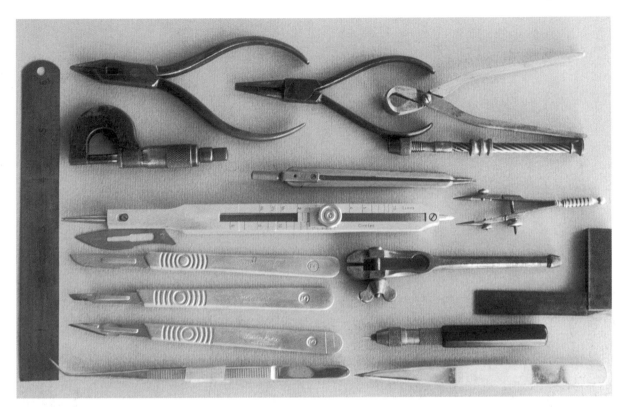

26 A selection of tools:
Left: 6in stainless steel rule with Imperial scales; metric scales on back.
Centre, bottom to top: tweezers with angled points; four Swann Morton replaceable surgical blades – No 11 pointed, No 15 small rounded end, No 10 medium rounded end (all on handles), and No 23 large rounded end; proportional dividers; micrometer; pin vice; milliner's pliers; round nose pliers.
Right, bottom to top: tweezers with straight points; Archimedean drill; square; pin chuck; spring bow dividers; end cutting pliers

Lighting

An angle-poise lamp gives satisfactory results, but it should be fitted with a long-life bulb rather than an ordinary tungsten one, as the former have minimal heat output. Halogen bulbs also give out far too much heat.

Ventilators

Cowl ventilators – the most common type – vary in trunk (stem) diameter from 9in to several feet. The diameter of the cowl is approximately 1.6 times the trunk diameter. The smaller sizes can be made by bending the head of a pin to lie at right angles to, and hard against, the stem. This is not as easy as it sounds (see Fig 18A, p42). Once the head has been turned, the convex top must be filed flat.

Another method, suitable for the larger sizes of ventilator, is to use spherical seeds, such as mustard or turnip. A seed should be cut in half with a razor blade, and have the pith removed. The shell thus formed is glued to the top of a

trunk the top of which has been cut at an angle to take the cowl. Paint will fill any slight gaps between cowl and stem.

The type of head shown in the diagram is also used (see Fig 18A). It can be made by holding a short piece of fine dowel, or cocktail stick in a pin vice and turning it to shape using a needle file whilst rotating the vice between finger and thumb. Mechanical ventilation units come in many types and sizes (see Figs 18A and B, pp42–3).

Water tanks

These are usually of cylindrical form, their length and diameter varying according to their purpose, and are supported by two bearers placed a short distance in from each end. They can be made from a piece of round wood or plastic rod.

Winches

Like a windlass, winches, and especially steam-driven winches, when seen from a short distance, can have the appearance

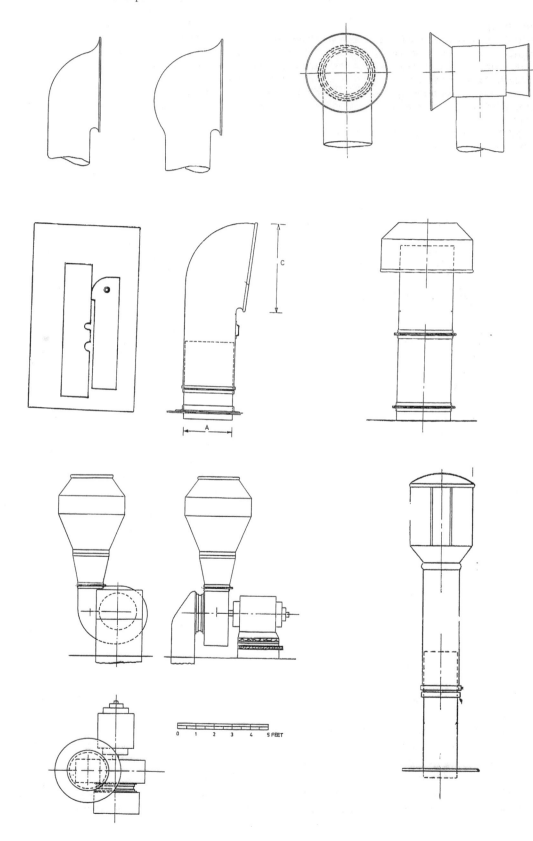

C

A

0 1 2 3 4 5 FEET

Figure 18A (left)
Above left: side view of two early forms of cowl ventilators; the mouth was circular.
Above right: a form of cowl that was found both as a standard ventilator and on the top of derrick posts.
Centre left: a simple, easily made jig to help when cutting seeds in half to form ventilator cowls. The arm on the right is moved sideways to allow a seed to be placed in one of the notches, and the arm closed and held against the seed. The seed is sliced in half with a razor blade by cutting down with the blade held against the fixed bar.
Centre: the standard form of cowl, where the diameter of the cowl (C) is approximately 1.6 times that of the diameter of the trunk (A).
Centre right: mushroom ventilator on which the diameter and height can vary to suit its application.
Below left: A typical mechanical ventilation unit.

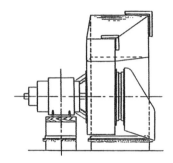

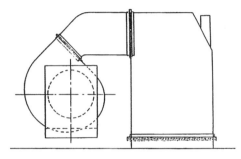

Figure 18B
Above and right: Another typical mechanical supply ventilation unit, the height and diameter of which can vary.
Below: the wrong way to turn the head of a pin to form a small cowl type ventilator (left) and the correct way (right). [Note: because of the wide variation in the heights and diameters of ventilators, no dimensions have been included. Plans will usually give an indication of these.]

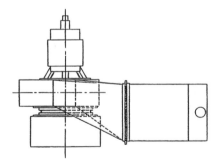

of a solid mass with a few protrusions. [Note: on the plans in Part II a winch has been indicated either as a rectangle with one or two small squares on each side to represent the warping drums, or as an L-shape with a single rectangle each side (the warping drums) to indicate the handing].

Electric winches are often handed (i.e. that on one side of the ship is a mirror image of that on the opposite side). A typical electric winch will comprise: base of 5ft 6in (1.67m) square, an overall height of 5ft (1.52m), lifting wire barrel of 24in (0.60m) diameter by 20in (0.50m) and long warp-

ing drums 18in (0.46m) diameter by 14in (0.36m) long. For a simple electric winch, cut a strip of thin card 0.015in thick by 0.55in wide (0.04mm x 1.4 mm). Mark off lengths of 0.55in along it. Lay a piece of plastic rod or wire 0.02in (0.5mm) diameter across one marked square so that the ends project 0.013in (0.34mm) each side. Glue a cylindrical piece of wood or plastic rod on one side at right angles to the wire (rod), with one end eased away where it crosses the wire. Do the same on every alternate square, handing them as necessary, for the number needed (plus a few spares), and

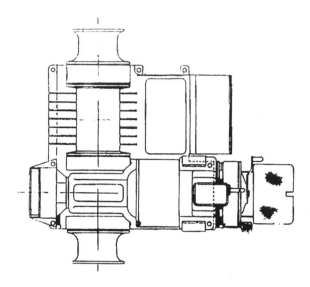

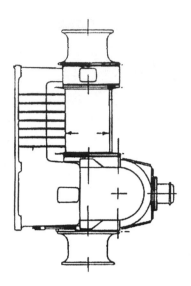

Figure 19A Plan of steam winch

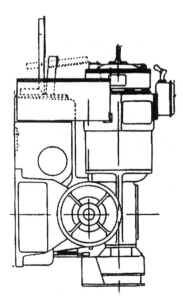

paint the whole strip. Part off each one, and touch up the cut edge of each base with a spot of paint.

Steam winches without the warping drums are about 6ft square and 3ft 6in high (2.0m x 1.0m), and the warping drums 15in (0.38m) long by 12in (0.30m) diameter. They can be made in quantity in the following way. Cut two strips of thin card (0.5mm thick) 0.60in (2mm) wide and on one strip mark off 0.60in length. Glue two short lengths of 0.015in (.05mm) diameter wire equally spaced across the marked length. Do the same on each alternate square along the length of the strip. When the glue is quite dry, place the strip upside down on a hard, smooth surface and but off the ends of the wire to leave only about 0.015in projecting each

side (a discarded Swann Morton blade can be used). Turn the strip right way up and glue the second strip on to it, making sure they are fully aligned, at the same time pressing down hard on the assembly. Any glue that is squeezed out must be removed before it sets hard. Paint the strip, part off the individual winches, and touch up the cut edges.

Warping winches are similar to the above, but have one set of warping drums on extended shafts, with a bearing support to the deck just inboard of the drum.

Windlass

The main parts of an anchor windlass comprise: a baseplate; four vertical frames to take shaft bearings; two cable lifting

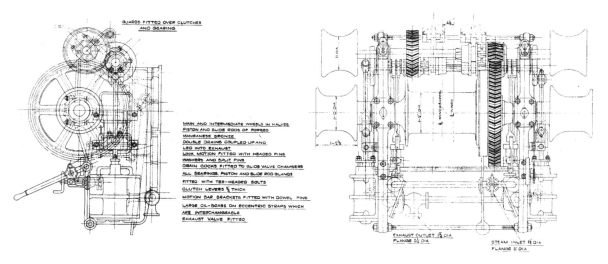

GUARDS FITTED OVER CLUTCHES
AND GEARING

MAIN AND INTERMEDIATE WHEELS IN HALVES
PISTON AND SLIDE RODS OF FORGED
MANGANESE BRONZE
DOUBLE DRAINS COUPLED UP AND
LED INTO EXHAUST
LINK MOTION FITTED WITH HEADED PINS
WASHERS AND SPLIT PINS
DRAIN COCKS FITTED TO SLIDE VALVE CHAMBERS
ALL BEARINGS, PISTON AND SLIDE ROD GLANDS
FITTED WITH TEE-HEADED BOLTS
CLUTCH LEVERS ⅝ THICK
MOTION BAR BRACKETS FITTED WITH DOWEL PINS
LARGE OIL-BOXES ON ECCENTRIC STRAPS WHICH
ARE INTERCHANGEABLE
EXHAUST VALVE FITTED

EXHAUST OUTLET 1⅝ DIA
FLANGE 3¼ DIA

STEAM INLET 1¾ DIA
FLANGE 5 DIA

ARRANGEMENT OF HORIZONTAL STEAM WINCH
CYLINDERS - 6" DIA × 10" STROKE

Figure 19B Plan of an electric winch

27A Electrically powered cargo winch

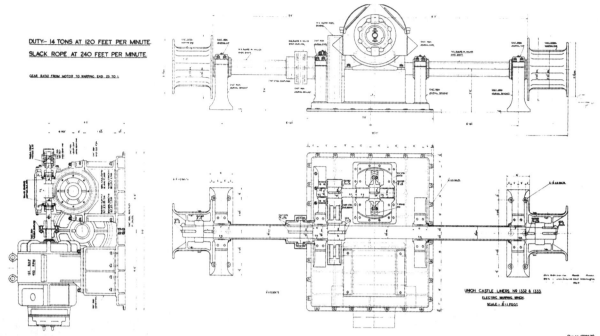

DUTY:- 14 TONS AT 120 FEET PER MINUTE.

SLACK ROPE AT 240 FEET PER MINUTE.

GEAR RATIO FROM MOTOR TO WARPING END 25 TO 1

UNION CASTLE LINERS Nº 1332 & 1333

ELECTRIC WARPING WINCH

SCALE ~ ⅜ = 1 FOOT

Figure 19C Plan of a warping winch

27B Side view of an electric cargo winch

drums; brake drums; a pair of warping drums; and either the steam cylinders or electric motor with their associated gearing. The size of a windlass depends upon the size of the anchor cable required for the size of ship.

As the baseplate will be about 0.13in x 0.085in (3.3x2mm) or less according to size, a simplified arrangement of this will be advisable. Cut a base and a pair of end plates from thin card and glue the latter to the outboard edges of the base. Form a pair of cable-lifting drums by turning from wood. Glue them to the inside of the end plates. Cut two larger card discs for the main gear wheels and glue one to the inner face of each cable-lifting drum. From thin card cut a pair of supports similar to the first pair, and glue one to the inner face of each of the gear wheel

discs. The warping drums can be turned from wood or plastic rod and glued in place on the outside of the end plates. If the windlass is driven by an electric motor, this can be made from a length of thin dowel, or plastic rod, with its diameter reduced by a third over half its length, placed fore and aft on the centre line at the after end of the windlass, with the reduced part between the two inner supports.

Should this appear too complicated there is an alternative method. As mentioned above, when viewed from a short distance some fittings painted in a dark or uniform colour may have a distinctive outline and shape but little discernible detail. To simulate this, carve a strip of wood so that in cross section it has the overall outline of the windlass when looked at from one end. After marking the overall width (excluding

27C Mooring Winch: showing warping drum on extended shaft.

28A Front view of a windlass

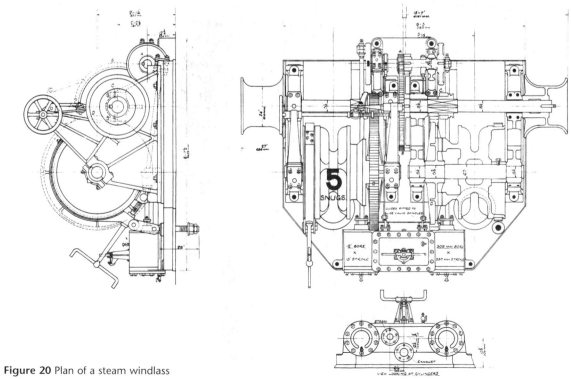

Figure 20 Plan of a steam windlass

28B Rear view of a windlass

the warping drums) carve the stick to the outline of the windlass as seen from the fore side and the after side. This should be done before cutting it away from the stick. Finally make and affix a warping drum at each end. After painting and fitting in place, put a short length of anchor chain (see Anchors, p11) between each hawse hole and the cable-lifter grooves on the windlass.

Windows

These can be marked in pencil as rectangles on the side of a deckhouse, etc, and filled with black ink, although this is a difficult and time-consuming job, in which it is difficult to obtain sharp corners. It is better to cut rectangles from black-painted cigarette paper and fix in place with clear matt varnish. As windows vary in size it is quicker to cut strips of the paper in the different window widths, and cut off pieces of the right length (height).

Part II

—

Ship Model Plans

—

1

Aorangi
(1924)

UNION STEAMSHIP COMPANY OF NEW ZEALAND

When she was completed in December 1924 for the Union Steamship Company of New Zealand, the *Aorangi* (the Maori name for Mount Cook) had the distinction of being the first, the largest and the fastest passenger liner in the world to be propelled solely by diesel engines. The ship (Yard No 603) was built by the Fairfield Shipbuilding & Engineering Co Ltd, Govan, Glasgow. The owners intended her for service on what was known as 'The All-Red Route' or, more prosaically, the run linking Sydney NSW, Auckland, New Zealand, Honolulu, the Fiji Islands and Vancouver in British Columbia. She remained on that route until the summer of 1941 when the Ministry of War Transport requisitioned her as a troop carrier. Just prior to the D-Day landings in Normandy she was fitted out to serve as a depot ship for servicing tugs and other auxiliary craft. Later that year she was converted to act as Commodore Ship for the Fleet Train for the British Pacific Fleet. She was handed back to her owners in 1946, who sent her to Sydney for overhaul and refitting for the trans-Pacific service. For various reasons it was not until September 1948 that she was ready to make her first voyage on that service. Being the only vessel on the route it soon became apparent that this was no longer an economic commercial undertaking, and the service was ended in 1953. *Aorangi* was laid up in Sydney and a short while later was sold to the British Iron and Steel Corporation, who allocated her to Arnott Young & Company's shipbreaking yard at Dalmuir on the Clyde, where she arrived under her own power at the end of July 1953. Thus she ended her career only a few miles downstream from the place where she was built. In all that time her original engines had given outstanding service.

Aorangi was a fine looking ship, with a nice sheer and open superstructure surmounted by two tall (although possibly a little on the slender side), well-raked funnels. The whole was set off by the company's livery of dark green hull

Specification	
Length overall:	600ft 0in (180m)
Length between perpendiculars (bp):	580ft 0in (175m)
Breadth moulded (mld):	72ft 0in (22.5m)
Draught:	27ft 6in (8.45m)
Tonnage, gross:	17,491
Machinery:	four 6-cyl Fairfield-Sulzer diesel engines = 13,000 bhp; quadruple screw
Speed:	18 knots
Passengers (as built):	440 first class, 300 second, 230 third

with a narrow yellow ribband, white superstructure and black-topped red funnels. The most noteworthy features of the ship were the four Fairfield-Sulzer engines, each developing 3250bhp, and which gave excellent service throughout the whole of the vessel's life.

Not unnaturally, the ship attracted a great deal of attention in the technical press at the time, and both *The Motor Ship* and *The Shipbuilder* carried lengthy articles fully illustrated with GA plans and a number of on-board photographs. Fortunately, many of the shipbuilder's original 'as fitted' drawings have survived. These include deck arrangements, lines, rig and a most superb 1/48-scale sectional profile. This plan, which is nearly 13ft (3.96m) long, offers incredible detail, right down to the turned legs of chairs and drawer handles. It is worth remembering that the plan was produced long before the introduction of today's tubular

The *Aorangi*

Photograph: author's collection

drawing pens and the multiplicity of templates and other drawing aids.

As a matter of passing interest, this was the second ship of the same name to be built at Fairfield, although when the first one was built in 1883 the company was known as John Elder & Co. This early vessel was a 389ft long, 4163 tons gross, barque-rigged, clipper stem, single-funnel steamer for the New Zealand Shipping Company.

Modelling Notes

It will be easier to carve the hull to the level of the Shelter Deck and to add the forecastle as a separate piece (its after end must be finished and painted before being fitted on the hull). Once that has been done the sides of the hull can be carved to shape. It is important to cut the sheer accurately. As the drawing shows, the sheer from midships aft is on the shallow side, a rise of 3ft 3in (1.0m), whereas from midships forward it is 9ft 9in (3.0m). The bow has quite a good flare with a bar stem, and the hull sides aft to the cruiser stern are moderately full in section. There is a bulwark along each side of the Shelter Deck from the break of the forecastle to a point just abaft the mainmast. It should be made from a

mounted shaving and fitted by the rebate method, taking care to ensure that the join is invisible after sanding.

The Promenade Deck overhangs the Shelter Deck by 18in (0.45m) each side over its whole length. The bulwark along each side can be glued to the edge of the deck card and the short lengths of full-height plating forward and aft can be cut integrally with the bulwark. The Boat Deck is of similar width, with only a short length of bulwark each side at the fore end.

The superstructure is straightforward, being made up of a number of houses. It is simpler to make the long deckhouses in several pieces, each piece being made to suit the changes in width along the house, rather than trying to embody the changes in width in a single long strip. Similarly, the bay windows should be added as separate pieces. The card for the Boat Deck will cover the butts, but it will be necessary to cover the Boat Deck house with paper to hide the butts.

As with liners of the period, there are quite a number of cowl ventilators of different sizes. As well as the large skylights adjacent to the funnels, there are several smaller skylights throughout the ship. The lifeboats are carried on

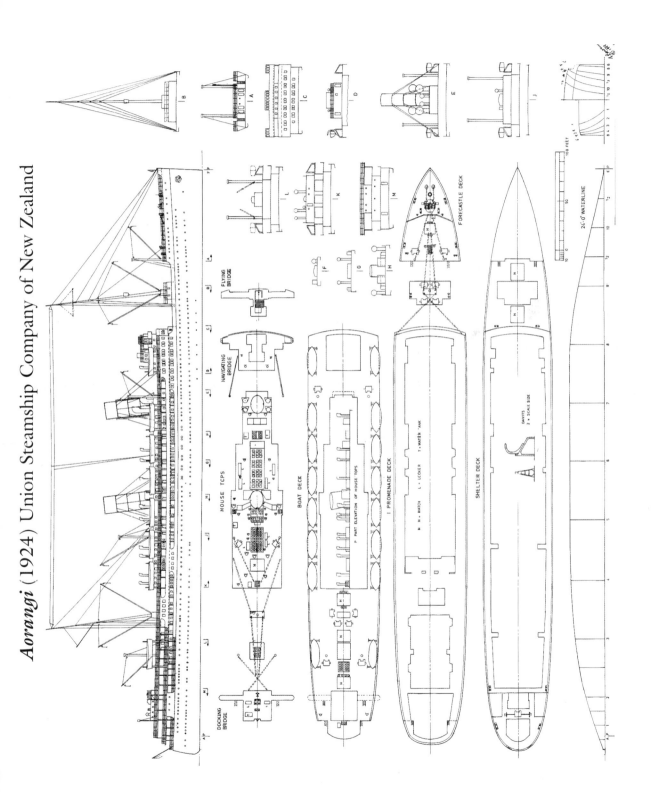

Aorangi (1924) Union Steamship Company of New Zealand

FLYING BRIDGE

NAVIGATING BRIDGE

HOUSE TOPS

BOAT DECK

PART ELEVATION OF HOUSE TOPS

I PROMENADE DECK

FORECASTLE DECK

SHELTER DECK

DOCKING BRIDGE

H = HATCH   L = LOCKER   T = WATER TANK

DAVITS
2 × SCALE SIZE

100 FEET

50

24'-0" WATERLINE

gravity davits, the inboard end of each trackway being supported by an 'A' frame. On the plan the cradles and boats have been omitted on many of the sections for clarity.

On the fore side of the after funnel are two large, shaped air intakes (best made solid). Just aft of these, on each side of the funnel, and running diagonally across the deck, is a rectangular (in cross-section) cover over a main exhaust pipe. It is about 5ft high and 3ft wide (1.5m and 0.9m). On the forecastle deck, outboard of the starboard derrick post, and set very close to it, is a galley funnel; this is 24ft (7.25m) high and about one third of the diameter of the derrick post.

Colour Scheme

Hull: Brunswick green (sometimes called Hooker's green) to the level of the Shelter Deck, white above; narrow yellow ribband at level of the Upper Deck; boot topping pinkish-red.

Superstructure: white; as built the wheelhouse was mahogany, but the lower half of the front was white to blend in with the white bulwarks of the Navigating Bridge.

Lifeboats and davits: white; boat covers light grey.

Masts, derrick posts, derricks: buff.
Ventilators: white, inside cowls red.
Windlass, winches: black.
Hatches: sides buff, tops light grey.
Funnels: Cunard red, black top, two narrow black bands.
Decks: all planked.
Miscellaneous: skylights white, breakwater white.

References

Illustrated articles with general arrangement plans (including a plan of the midship section): *The Shipbuilder* (January 1925); *The Motor Ship* (January 1925).

The Glasgow City Archives (see Appendix II, pp 205–206) have many 'as fitted' and other plans of the ship. They have also a considerable number of excellent photographs of the vessel, including external and on-board deck shots. See also *Sea Breezes*, Volume 49 (August issue): J H Isherwood's 'Steamers of the Past' series.

For a more general reference to the Union Steamship Company: *Glamour Ships of the Union Steamship Company of New Zealand* by Jack Churchouse (Wellington, New Zealand: Millwood Press Ltd, 1981).

2

Athenia
(1923)

ANCHOR-DONALDSON LINE

*A*thenia was completed in Glasgow in 1923 by the Fairfield Shipbuilding & Engineering Co Ltd, Govan, for the Anchor-Donaldson Line (which later became the Donaldson Atlantic Line), also of Glasgow. *Athenia* (Yard No 596) and her sister ship *Letitia* (also from the Fairfield Company, Yard No 601, in 1924), were familiar sights to Clydesiders in the 1920s and 1930s as they sailed on the owner's service between Glasgow and Canada.

When World War II started *Athenia* was on a voyage from Glasgow and Liverpool to Montreal. On 3 September 1939, only seven hours after the British Government had declared war on Germany, a U-Boat torpedoed the vessel. Although remaining afloat until the following day, 93 passengers and 19 crew were lost.

Her sister ship *Letitia* survived the war and was sold to the Ministry of Transport in 1946, renamed *Empire Brent* and used as a troopship and later as an immigrant ship on the Australian run. After an extensive overhaul in 1952 she was chartered to the New Zealand Government for service

as an immigrant ship and renamed *Captain Cook*. Eight years later, in 1960, she was sold to shipbreakers and broken up at Inverkeithing, Scotland.

The two ships were almost identical in appearance. Initially they could be distinguished by the windows in the steel screen on the side of the Promenade Deck immediately below the first boat each side on the Boat Deck above. On *Athenia* the two windows were closely spaced, but on *Letitia* they were much wider apart. Later, probably at some time in the 1930s, part of the Promenade Deck on *Athenia* immediately abaft the above screen was plated in and five more windows added. Aft, the existing open sides of the Bridge Deck were plated in and the after end of the Promenade Deck extended aft for some 24ft (7.25m).

Modelling Notes

The plan is for the ship as built. The hull can be made to the line of the Bridge Deck and cut down at the after end to the level of the Shelter Deck. The bow has quite a pronounced flare and, as can be seen on the body plan, the ship's side at the after end, where it runs round to the cruiser stern, is almost flat with only very little curvature.

The superstructure and various houses should not present any difficulties. If the long midship house on the Bridge Deck is made slightly smaller in width than the hull block it can be faced with a piece of paper-mounted shaving, extended upwards to form the bulwark along the Promenade Deck, together with the plate screen at either end, and cut to form the short bulwark on the Bridge Deck forward of the bridge front. Similarly at the after end it can be cut to form the short bulwark along the Bridge Deck and the curtain plate to the Promenade Deck. Except for the forward and after boats each side on the Boat Deck the rest of the boats are of the nested arrangement, i.e. a 28ft (8.5m) boat is stowed inside a 30ft (9.14m) boat.

Specification

Length overall:	538ft 2in (164.03m)
Length bp:	520ft 0in (158.45m)
Breadth:	66ft 0in (20.12m)
Draught:	27ft 8in (8.43m)
Tonnage, gross:	12,000 tons
Machinery:	Steam turbines, 8700 shp, twin screw
Speed:	15 knots
Passengers:	516 cabin class, 972 third

Athenia in the Clyde in 1938. This shows some of the changes mentioned in the text.   *Photograph: author's collection*

Athenia from the starboard quarter.   *Photograph: J Clarkson*

Athenia (1923) Anchor-Donaldson Line

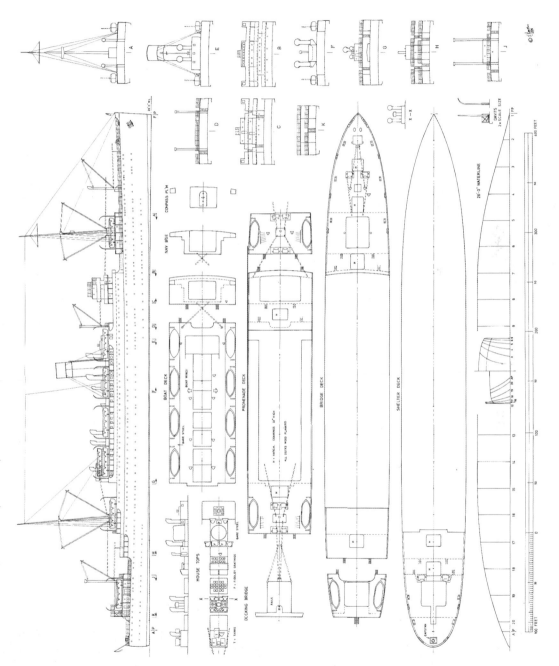

Photographs of the ship taken at different times during her life show variations in the number of boats and their stowage positions. The funnel seems to be slightly on the thin side for a vessel of this size, and is thus a characteristic of her overall appearance, so care must be taken to avoid making it too large.

Colour Scheme

Hull: black above waterline to the level of the Bridge Deck, boot topping red. At some time, possibly around 1935, a narrow white band was added dividing the black from the red boot topping.

Superstructure: white; deckhouses white.

Masts, derrick posts, derricks: medium grey.

Hatches: coamings buff, tops grey.

Lifeboats, davits: white, with grey covers; davits white.

Ventilators: large cowl ventilators on engine and boiler casing, i.e. on house-tops, black; all other cowl ventilators medium grey; inside of all cowls red.

Decks: all decks wood planked; decks under lifeboats bare steel (grey) for width of 10ft in from ship's side; deck under winches bare steel (grey), shown by rectangular outline; top of boiler casing, in way of funnel, grey.

Windlass: black.

Winches: black.

Capstans: black.

Bollards, fairleads: black.

Funnel: black, with broad white band.

Miscellaneous: water tanks buff; inside bulwarks white.

References

Glasgow City Archives (for contact details see Appendix II, pp 205–206) have a number of the shipbuilder's original plans, including rigging plan, general arrangements of all decks, midship section, body plan to loft offsets, shell expansion, ventilation plans. They have a number of photographs of the ship: two on the building berth, one at the bow and one at the stern taken just prior to the launch; two on trials; and three useful on-board deck views. They have a similar holding of plans and photographs for the *Letitia*.

Shipbuilding & Shipping Record (12 July 1923) includes an illustrated article about the ship, accompanied by small-scale but well-detailed external profile and general arrangement plans of all decks.

There is a large and highly detailed shipbuilder's scale model of the ship in the Museum of Transport, Glasgow.

For general history of the company: *The Donaldson Line 1854/1954* by Alistair Dunnett (Glasgow: Jackson Son & Co, 1960); *Donaldson Line* by P J Telford (Kendal: World Ship Society, 1989).

3

Avila

(1927)

BLUE STAR LINE

In 1925 the Blue Star Line (1920) Ltd placed orders for nine vessels with shipyards in the United Kingdom. These were liners for a UK to South America passenger service, this being the first time that the company had entered that particular trade.

Three ships, *Almeda*, *Andalucia* and *Arandora*, were built by Cammell Laird & Co Ltd, Birkenhead, and two, *Avila* (Yard No 514) and *Avelona*, (Yard No 515) by John Brown & Co Ltd, Clydebank. All five were completed in 1926–27 and were generally similar in external appearance, though there were some minor differences between the Birkenhead and Clydebank ships, as will be noted later. In 1929, to avoid further confusion with the Royal Mail Steam Packet Company's 'A' class ships, the word *Star* was added as a suffix to their names. The conspicuous cowl tops fitted to their funnels were removed in 1928. The after funnel on all five vessels was a dummy.

In 1935 the *Almeda Star* and *Andalucia Star* were lengthened by some 65ft (19.8m) and fitted with a Maierform bow. The *Avila Star* was treated similarly, but in her case the increase in length was only about 38ft (11.6m).

Because of changing trade conditions the *Avelona Star* was withdrawn in 1934 and rebuilt as a cargo-only vessel with the after funnel and the upper decks being removed. The fifth ship *Arandora* was sent to the Fairfield yard on the Clyde in 1928 and extensively refitted as a cruise liner. Renamed *Arandora Star* upon completion of the work in 1929, she became a very popular cruise ship in the years leading up to the outbreak of World War II. The Blue Star Line fleet suffered heavy losses during the war, and all five of these vessels were among the ships lost through enemy action.

Modelling Notes

The plans are of the ship as built. As there are only two short well decks it is better to carve the sheer to the level of the forecastle/bridge deck/poop, and then cut out the wells down to the level of the Upper Deck. However, there is one point to note: the height of the Bridge Deck above the Upper Deck, from its fore end back to the bridge front, increases from 8ft 6in to 11ft 6in (2.6m to 3.5m). At the after end abaft the superstructure it is 8ft 6in (2.6m). The best way to deal with this, since the sheer line of the hull block has been cut to the 8ft 6in level throughout, is to add a piece of wood 0.03in (0.9mm) – or 3ft (0.9m) to scale – to the Bridge Deck in this area. With this done, the hull block can be carved to shape. It has an easy flare, and note that the ship is fitted with a bar (not a rolled plate) stem.

The superstructure is a straightforward assembly of the individual pieces that represent its constituent parts. Where appropriate these are reduced in thickness by the thickness of the card being used for the overhanging decks with curtain plates. However, there are one or two points to note. On the Boat Deck there is a raised area 18in (0.45m) high, which is wood planked except where it extends under the after funnel when it is bare steel. The house at the forward

Specification

Length overall:	530ft 6in (161.69m)
Length bp:	510ft 0in (155.45m)
Breadth:	68ft 0in (20.72m)
Draught:	27ft 6in (8.38m)
Tonnage, gross:	12,872 tons
Machinery:	4 steam turbines with single reduction gear to 2 shafts
Speed:	17 knots

Avila as completed.

Photograph: author's collection

end of the Upper Promenade Deck is 10ft (3.05m) high, but there is a narrow raised casing 18in (0.45m) high above the Upper Promenade Deck along each side (see section D on the plan). The house immediately below this one on the Promenade Deck has a bay window each side. It is easier to add these as separate pieces after the rectangular piece forming the house has been cut.

As completed, these ships had cowl-topped funnels. The method of making them is given in the entry for funnels in Part I (see p25). The cowls were later removed. There were

Port quarter view of the *Avila* as built.

Photograph: author's collection

two waste steam pipes on the after end of each funnel. These were set about 3ft (0.9m) on either side of the centre line, and were painted to match the funnel colours.

The rake of the mainmast is greater than that of the foremast, while that of the funnels is between the two. Here the foremast rake is 5 degrees and that of the mainmast 6 degrees.

As mentioned above, there were several small differences in the external appearance of the Birkenhead and Clydebank ships as built. The four pairs of large cowl ventilators in way of the funnels were the same height and whereas they were painted white on the Birkenhead ships, they were black on the Clydebank pair, with the forward pair some 6ft (1.8m) higher than the others. Later, when the cowl tops were removed from the funnels, it would seem that the white cowl ventilators were painted black, and the pair forward of the fore funnel increased in height by some 7ft (2.1m). On the three Cammell Laird ships there are 17 stanchions between the top of the Promenade Deck bulwark and the Upper Promenade Deck, and 11 between the Upper Promenade Deck and the Boat Deck. On the John Brown vessels there are only 12 and 8 respectively. On the *Avila* and *Avelonna* where the corner of the bridge front superstructure plating meets the Upper Deck, the side plating is cut back in a curve between the Promenade Deck and the Upper Promenade Deck. On the other three ships this corner of the bridge front superstructure plating and the side

plating runs right down to the deck. This can be seen on the photograph of the *Almeda*, below.

There is one other point to note about the Birkenhead ships: in contrast to the figures given above, records show their length between perpendiculars as 512ft and overall length as 535ft. It has not been possible to find out where these slight differences in dimensions have been incorporated into the Laird-built hulls.

Colour Scheme

Hull: black to the level of the top of the Upper Deck bulwark, white above; boot topping red with narrow white dividing line.

Superstructure: white.

Masts, derrick posts, derricks: buff.

Ventilators: white; four pairs of cowl ventilators adjacent to funnels, black; inside of cowls red (see also notes in text).

Windlass, winches, bollards, fairleads: black.

Hatches: black.

Skylights, water tanks, potato locker, rails, etc: white.

Boats, davits: white, with light canvas covers.

Funnel: orange-red, with black top, thin white band, thin black band (all touching); white disc with blue five-pointed star in center – position as shown on the plan; waste steam pipes painted to correspond to funnel colours; cowls black.

Decks: wood sheathed; bare steel decks where marked, black; waterways red oxide.

This photo of the *Almeda*, one of the three Cammell Laird ships, has been included to show some of the variations between the two groups of ships. Points to notice are the height of the cowl ventilators by the funnels and their colour, the increased number of deck stanchions between the Bridge/Promenade/Boat Decks, and the sharp angle where the front of the superstructure meets the Deck.

Photograph: author's collection

Avila (1927) Blue Star Line

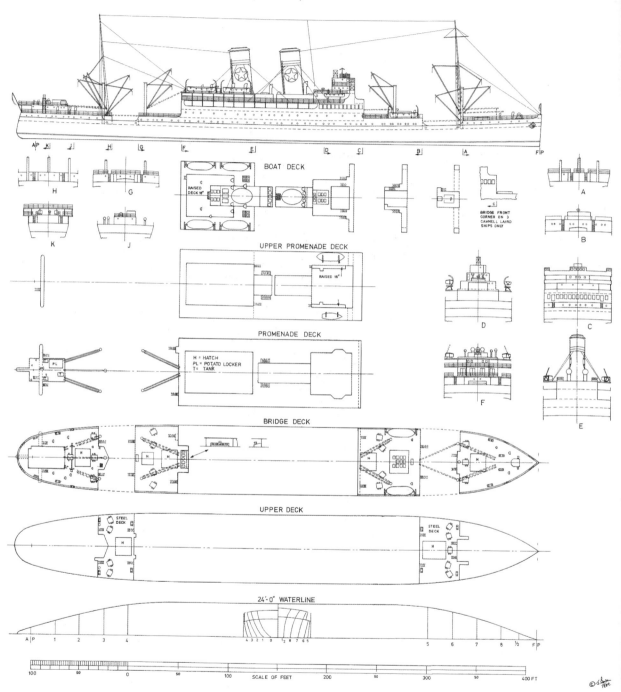

References

Shipbuilder's plans of the ship are held by Glasgow University Business Records Centre (see Appendix II, pp205–206). *Blue Star* by Tony Atkinson & Kevin O'Donoghue (World Ship Society, 1985) is a general history of the company, with a list of its ships (many illustrated).

4

Braemar Castle (1952)

UNION-CASTLE LINE

The *Braemar Castle* was the last of a quartet of one-class passenger liners ordered by the Union-Castle Line around 1950 for their Round Africa service from the UK. She and her sister ships *Kenya Castle* and *Rhodesia Castle* were almost identical, but differed from the first ship of the quartet, *Bloemfontein Castle*, in that they were turbine powered whereas the latter was fitted with diesel machinery. In addition, the *Bloemfontein Castle* was some 20ft longer, had 2ft more beam, and was fitted with only a single mast set abaft the bridge, with a pair of derrick posts in place of the mainmast carried by the other three ships.

All four of the Castle vessels were built by Harland & Wolff Ltd in Belfast. *Braemar Castle* was completed towards the end of 1952, and sailed from London on her maiden voyage in November of that year. She would seem to have had an uneventful life. In about 1960–61 the funnel was increased in height by the fitting of a dome top, but after barely fourteen years of service she was sold for scrap and arrived at Faslane on the Gareloch, Scotland in January 1966.

Modelling Notes

These intermediate liners were good-looking vessels, and with their uncluttered decks and attractive colour scheme make good subjects for miniature models. The plans are for the *Braemar Castle* as built.

The hull can be carved to the level of C (Bridge) Deck, and cut down aft to the level of B (Shade) Deck. This is built up in the usual way, with a deck card of sufficient thickness to represent the curtain plate along the edge of the after end of C Deck. The hull has a well-raked, straight-rolled plate stem and a nice easy flare. The bulwark at the fore end of C Deck is slightly knuckled at the deck line for the after half of its length, which brings it more upright. As the drawing shows, the after end of the hull is fairly full in plan view and

Specification	
Length overall:	576ft 6in (175.76m)
Length bp:	540ft 0in (164.59m)
Breadth mld:	74ft 0in (22.5m)
Draught:	28ft 2in (8.55m)
Tonnage, gross:	17,040 tons
Machinery:	geared turbines, 14,400 shp, twin screw
Speed:	17 knots
Passengers:	530 in one class

with well-curved sides.

The superstructure and deckhouses are straightforward, with the fore end being covered with paper carried up to form the bulwark across the fore end of the Boat Deck. The boats are carried in gravity davits and are stowed fairly high above the deck to allow plenty of headroom for the passengers. Coamings are only found on Nos 1 and 2 hatches on C Deck forward. The covers of the other three hatches are flush with the deck planking to provide an uncluttered open deck space. Note the swimming pool on C Deck aft. All derricks are stowed horizontally but parallel to the sheer, except for the heavy derrick which is stowed vertically on the after side of the foremast.

Colour Scheme

Hull: Union-Castle lavender grey to level of the top of B Deck bulwark, white above, with narrow 4in (10cm) teak colour dividing line; boot topping red. There does not appear to be a single colour in the modelmakers' available

Braemar Castle as completed.

Photograph: author's collection

ranges of paints that is the exact shade of Lavender grey. Humbrol paints mixed in the following proportions will produce an acceptable result: 10 parts No 147 Light Grey, 1 part No 174 Signal Red, 2 parts No 104 Blue.

Superstructure, deckhouses, inside bulwarks: white.

Decks: all wood sheathed; steel deck in way of funnel mid grey.

Windlass, winches, bollards, fairleads: mid-grey.

Hatches: mid-grey.

Masts: red-brown.

Derrick posts, derricks: white, but heavy derrick mast colour.

Skylights, vent units, etc: white.

Funnel: vermilion (orange-red), black top.

References

Technical articles, with small-scale plans are available for all four Castle vessels. For *Braemar Castle*: *Shipping World* (3 December 1952). For *Bloemfontein Castle*: *Shipbuilder & Marine Engine-Builder* (June 1950); *Shipbuilding & Shipping Record* (6 April 1950); *Shipping World* (12 April 1950); *Motor Ship* (April/May 1950). For *Kenya Castle*: *Shipbuilder & Marine Engine-Builder* (July 1952). For *Rhodesia Castle*: *Shipbuilding & Shipping Record* (17 January 1952).

For general reference to the ships of the Union-Castle Line: *The Cape Run* by WH Mitchell & LA Sawyer (Lavenham, Suffolk: Terence Dalton, 1984); *Mailships of the Union-Castle Line* by C J Harris & Brian Ingpen (Patrick Stephens, 1994).

Braemar Castle (1952) Union-Castle Line

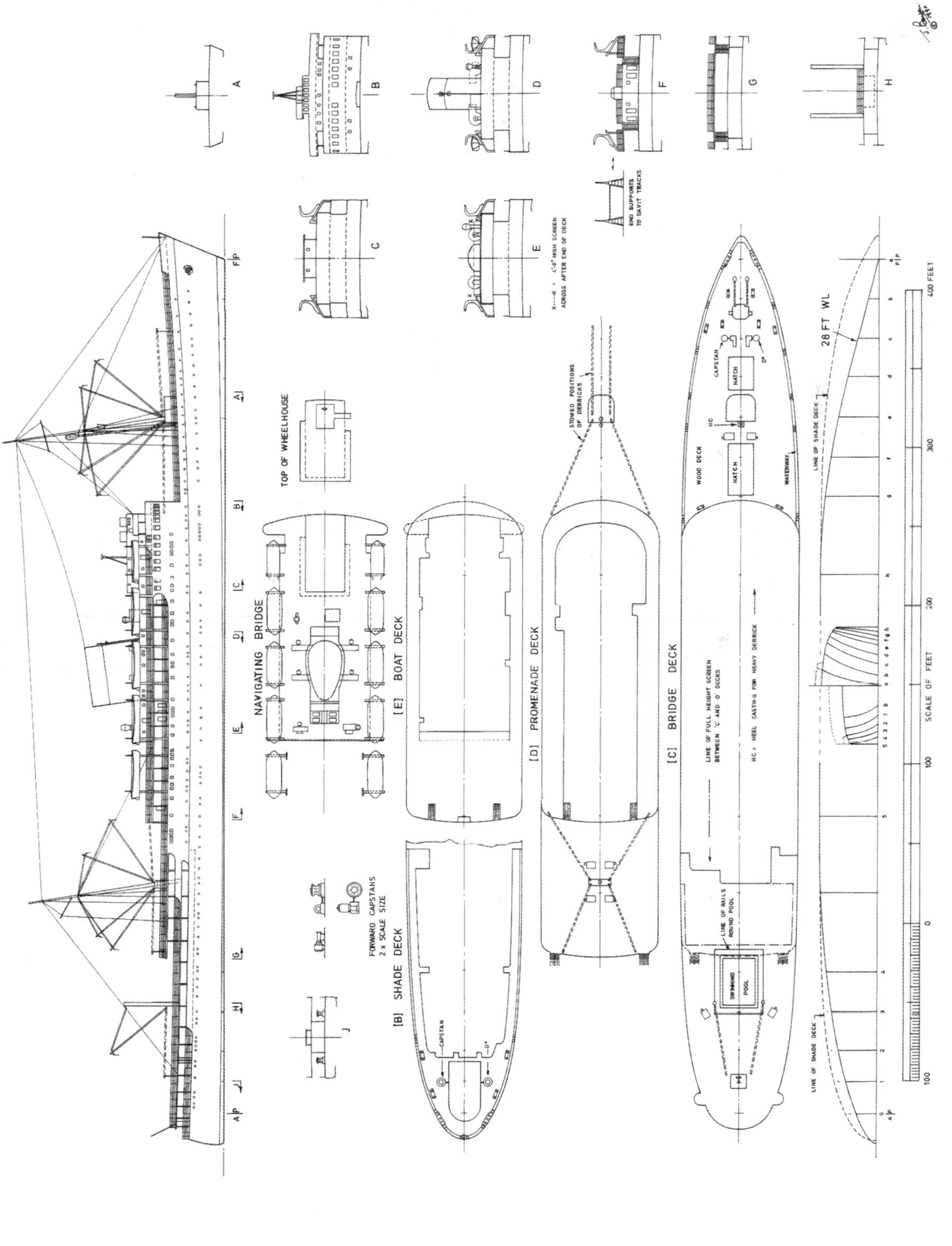

TOP OF WHEELHOUSE

NAVIGATING BRIDGE

[E] BOAT DECK

[D] PROMENADE DECK

[C] BRIDGE DECK

[B] SHADE DECK

FORWARD CAPSTANS
2 x SCALE SIZE

CAPSTAN

SWIMMING POOL

LINE OF RAILS ROUND POOL

LINE OF FULL HEIGHT SCREEN
BETWEEN 'C' AND 'D' DECKS

HC = HEEL CASTING FOR HEAVY DERRICK

WOOD DECK

HATCH

HATCH

CAPSTAN

WATERWAY

STOWED POSITIONS OF DERRICKS

X----X = 4'-6" HIGH SCREEN
ACROSS AFTER END OF DECK

END SUPPORTS
TO DAVIT TRACKS

28 FT WL

LINE OF SHADE DECK

LINE OF SHADE DECK

SCALE OF FEET

FP

AP

FP

AP

A B C D E F G H J

100 200 300 400 FEET

0 100

5

HMHS *Britannic* (1914)

WHITE STAR LINE

HOSPITAL SHIP

Even as the White Star Line's magnificent new liner *Olympic* was making her successful and acclaimed entry into the Company's Southampton to New York service in 1911, and her sister ship *Titanic* was nearing completion in Harland & Wolff's yard in Belfast, the White Star Line was having discussions with Harland & Wolff about the need to build a third liner of the class to counter the competition arising from similar large ships being built by the Cunard Line and the German Hamburg-Amerika Line.

The outcome of these talks was that the White Star Line placed an order with Harland & Wolff in June 1911 for a third ship, the *Britannic*. For various reasons work on the new ship, which was basically a repeat of the previous pair,

was slow in getting under way. As it turned out this was quite fortuitous. Because the ship was only in the very early stages of construction, the owners were able to incorporate a number of changes in the design after recommendations arising from the *Titanic* disaster. The major structural alterations to the hull increased the beam to 94ft (27.2m). Externally the most noticeable differences lay in the new methods of launching the lifeboats, and at the after end of the hull, where the Shelter Deck was now enclosed. The opportunity was also taken to make some minor alterations to the passenger accommodation and facilities, and add some improvements following seagoing experience on the *Olympic*.

HMHS *Britannic*   *Photograph: author's collection*

So work progressed and *Britannic* was launched on 14 February 1914. However, internal problems within the yard again caused delays, which were further increased when war broke out in August 1914 and the yard became heavily involved with war work. Although merchant work became a low priority, some progress was made on the new liner.

Then, in 1915 the appalling casualties from the Dardanelles campaign were placing a heavy strain on the facilities for transporting the wounded, and in mid-November the partially completed *Britannic* was requisitioned for use as a hospital ship. Immediately work was put in hand to complete the liner for her new role, and in just four weeks she was ready. At the time of requisition, only five of the projected eight huge gantries for handling the lifeboats had been fitted. It was decided not to fit the other three, and instead six lifeboats, each with a collapsible stowed underneath, were fitted along both sides of the Boat Deck. Ordinary Welin quadrant davits were fitted to handle the boats. A further lifeboat with collapsible below, was fitted on each side of the Poop. An additional deckhouse was added right at the after end of the Shelter Deck to act as a mortuary. The ship was, of course, painted in the standard hospital ship livery of white hull and upperworks, yellow-buff funnels, and with a broad green ribband along each side of the hull interrupted in three places by large red crosses.

HMHS *Britannic* made a number of voyages to Southampton with casualties from the Dardanelles, but on the morning of 21 November 1916, when on her way through the Kea Channel to Mudros, she struck a mine and sank very quickly, with the loss of 29 lives.

Sources

Few shipbuilder's plans of the *Britannic* appear to exist, excepting a sectional profile and general arrangement (GA) plans of all decks except the House Tops. These 1/12-scale drawings appear to be what are called design plans, and as such lack much in the way of essential detail of deck fittings, particularly of ventilation gear. There is, too, a 1/144-scale rigging plan, which included a useful seagull's-eye plan view of the ship. This went some way to solving several of the queries caused by the lack of a general arrangement drawing of the House Tops. No other drawings appear to exist for the ship, and the above-mentioned 'design' plans are those found in recent books about the ship, and in the articles published in technical journals at the time of her launch.

Because of her short life, there are not all that many photographs of the ship after completion. The Ulster Folk and Transport Museum in Belfast have a large number of photographs of the ship and her machinery taken whilst she was

Specification	
Length overall:	882ft 9in (269.06m)
Length bp:	850ft 0in (259.08m)
Breadth mld:	94ft 0in (28.65m)
Draught (design), full load:	34ft 0in (10.36m)
Tonnage, gross:	48,158 tons
Machinery:	triple expansion engines, 32,000 ihp; low-pressure turbine, 18,000shp; triple screw
Speed:	21 knots

being built, but very few (and no on board deck shots) of her on completion. The Imperial War Museum has a number of photographs of her, as have the National Maritime Museum, Greenwich, and the Southampton Maritime Museum. Beken of Cowes has at least one fine port side view.

The technical journals *Engineering* and *The Shipbuilder* published articles about the construction of the ship at the time of her launch. Several books published in the last few years cover the ship in some depth (see References).

There appears to be some confusion about the length (not overall length), which is at times given as 850ft and sometimes as 852ft 9in. In fact both are right, provided they are accompanied by the appropriate designation. The figure of 850ft is the between perpendiculars distance from the fore side of the stem to the after face of the sternpost (or centre of rudder stock if there is no sternpost) at the summer load waterline. The figure of 852ft 9in is the length from the fore part of the stem at the uppermost continuous deck (at this time the Certificate of Registration included the words 'under the bowsprit' here) to the after side of the head of the sternpost, and this is the figure for length entered on the ship's Certificate of Registration, made out at the time of completion. Any difference between the two figures will be due to the rake of the stem. The builders confirmed that the bp length was 850ft.

As noted earlier, information about this ship is somewhat limited. The drawing has been based on the above plans, with further detail added following a close study of available photographs. In some places where it was deemed suitable a number of details, mainly ventilation arrangements, have been based on those of her sister ships, since in general internal layouts were very similar.

Modelling Notes

It is essential to get the somewhat shallow curve of the sheer correct, and to carve the shape of the counter stern accurately, otherwise the character of the vessel will be lost.

The hull block should be cut to the level of the forecastle, Bridge Deck and poop, cutting away the forward well to the level of the Shelter Deck. The well deck bulwarks can be fitted by the rebate method after the sides of the hull have been carved to shape. The opening aft each side in way of the Shelter Deck can be cut as a slot about ⅜₆in deep, with the bottom at Shelter Deck level, and the top the depth of the Bridge Deck curtain plate below the edge of that deck. The bulwark can be fitted by the rebate method. It helps if the deck stanchions in way (note that the middle one is double width) are cut to length and glued to the inside of the bulwark before it is fitted. Remember to paint the inside of the slots white before fitting the bulwarks.

For the superstructure the heights of the deckhouses, and of the erections on the Boat Deck, are shown on the sectional profile. There is a bulwark along each side of the Promenade Deck and the Boat Deck. The stanchions between these decks were equally spaced at 9ft (2.7m) intervals, but additional stanchions were fitted in way of the lifeboat gantries with a short tie plate at the top.

The large gantries handling the lifeboats are of lattice construction, with the curved part at the top plated over and with a small plated area at the heel. The way in which these are to be made is best left to the ingenuity of the modeller! When fitted on the model they should not be set vertically but angled inboard, with the top directly above the innermost boat below it. Along each side of the Boat Deck are six 34ft (10.3m) lifeboats, each with a collapsible stowed on deck below it. Each of the lifeboats is stowed on a pair of pedestals with the keel just above the level of the top of the bulwark. The boat davits are of the Welin quadrant type and, unlike those on the *Titanic* where a single frame had a davit arm on each side, here each arm has its own frame. There are no boats forward on the port side of the deck where the original port gantry would have been fitted. On the poop there is another 34ft lifeboat, with a collapsible stowed on deck below it, each side. Again, the lifeboats are stowed on pedestals and handled by Welin quadrant davits.

On the forecastle two cable lifters are fitted to handle the anchors and there are four mooring capstans, a breakwater, cargo hatch and three electric winches. A single derrick is fitted on the after side of the foremast and is stowed against the mast. The jibs on the two cargo-handling cranes in the forward well are slightly shorter than those on the four cranes aft.

The locations of the various ventilation units are shown on the plan, as are the details of the individual types. For clarity the windows on the sides of the deckhouse in way of the open section of the Bridge Deck and Promenade Deck are shown on the sectional profile.

Note that the two red crosses each side on the superstructure are separate units hung outside the bulwarks. They should not be painted on the superstructure.

Colour Scheme

Hull: white above waterline, red below; broad green ribband, broken where shown by three large red crosses.
Superstructure, deckhouses: white; inside bulwarks white.
Gantries: yellow-buff, as funnels.
Lifeboats, davits: white, dark brown gunwale on lifeboats; covers light grey, no side tabs.
Cable lifters, capstans: black.
Winches, hatches: light grey.
Cranes: white.
Ventilation units, ventilators: white.
Bollards, fairleads: black.
Funnels: yellow-buff.
Decks: all wood planked.

References

HMHS Britannic: The Last of the Titans by Simon Mills (Waterfront Publications, 1992 [ISBN 0-946184-71-2]) of which a revised edition from 1998 is now available; *Titanic and her sisters Olympic & Britannic* (PRC Publications Ltd, 1998 [ISBN 0-68107-612-7]); *The Anatomy of the Titanic* by Tom McClusky (PRC Publications Ltd, 1998 [ISBN 1-85648-4823]), which, although not directly concerned with the *Britannic*, is about the best of the many recent publications on the subject as it concentrates on the construction of the ship and its basic history and contains numerous photographs. It is also useful for constructional details of the class.

Engineering (27 February 1914) includes an article that covers construction of the *Britannic* up to her launch; *The Shipbuilder* No 43 (March 1914) provides a similar, although shorter, article to the above. This article is reproduced in 'Distinguished Liners' from *The Shipbuilder* 1907–1914, Volume 2, compiled and edited by Mark D Warren (New York: Blue Riband Publications, Inc, 1997 [ISBN 0-9648153-1-1]).

Photographs: Ulster Folk & Transport Museum; Imperial War Museum; National Maritime Museum; Southampton Maritime Museum; Beken Maritime Services. For contact details see Appendix II, pp205–206.

HMHS *Britannic* (1914) White Star Line · Hospital Ship

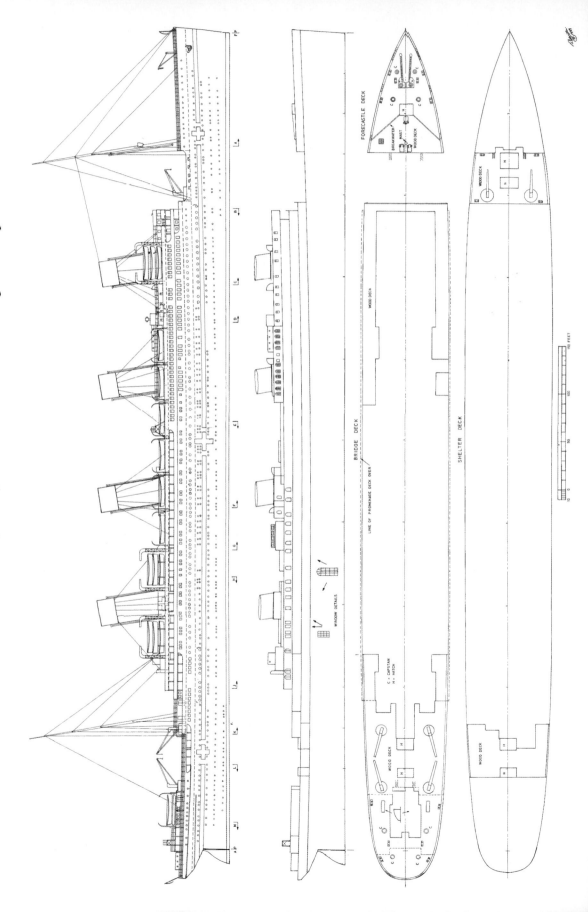

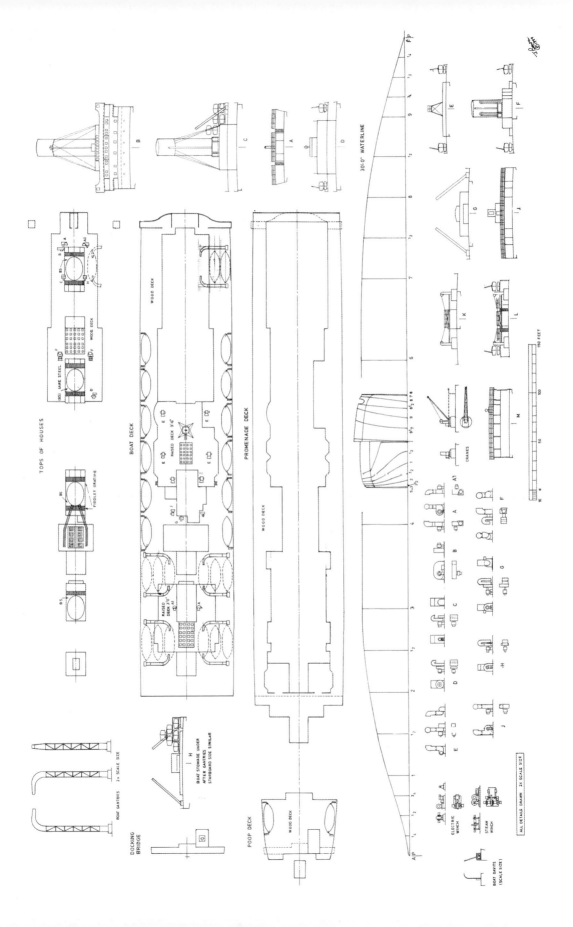

6

Britannic
(1930)

WHITE STAR LINE

*B*ritannic was the first diesel powered ship to be ordered by the White Star Line, and was followed two years later by a sister ship, *Georgic*. They were built by Harland & Wolff in Belfast and were intended for the company's Liverpool to New York service. The two could always be told apart because the latter had a rounded front to the superstructure, whereas that of the former was square. At the end of August 1939 *Britannic* was requisitioned for service as a troopship, and served in that capacity until released and handed back to her owners in 1947. They sent her to Liverpool where she was given a thorough overhaul and refitted as a two-class ship after which she returned to service from that port to New York. She remained on that run, but with some cruising during the winter months, until withdrawn at the end of 1960. She was sold for scrap and broken up at Inverkeithing, Scotland.

The most noticeable external change in her appearance from the 1947 overhaul was the plating in of the open sides to the Bridge Deck and the remaining open sides of the Promenade Deck below the Boat Deck, and the fitting therein of large glazed windows. With her flat-topped, (i.e. parallel to the waterline) funnels and long, low profile, *Britannic* introduced a new look to the owner's fleet. Although perhaps not to everyone's taste, many felt that she was a fine, good-looking vessel.

Modelling Notes

The hull is best made to the level of A Deck (forecastle deck), and cut down at the after end to B Deck. Once the sides of the hull have been carved to shape, the opening on each side forward to B Deck can be made. These can be formed as slots cut to the line of B Deck, but without cutting away at A Deck to leave this solid and of a thickness equal to the depth of the curtain plate. The bulwark, cut from a piece of mounted shaving, should be fitted by the

Specification	
Length overall:	712ft 0in (217.0m)
Length bp:	680ft 0in (207.3m)
Breadth mld:	82ft 0in (25.0m)
Draught:	32ft 9in (9.98m)
Tonnage, gross:	26,943 tons
Machinery:	two 10-cylinder 4-stroke double acting diesels, 20,000shp; twin screw
Speed:	17 knots
Passengers, as built:	504 cabin class, 551 tourist, 498 third

rebate method. It will be easier to glue the deck stanchions to the inside of the bulwark strips before they are fitted. The recesses can be made about 5mm deep and should be painted white before the bulwark pieces are fitted. All work on B Deck aft must be completed at this stage, i.e. deck painted, houses finished complete with doors and windows, fittings installed. This is necessary since part of this area will need to be covered by the card that forms the after end of the deck.

The rest of the superstructure is built up from a number of deckhouses and deck cards. The Boat Deck overhangs the Promenade Deck by 18in (0.45m) [or 0.4mm in scale] each side. On the House Tops there is a raised area 2ft (0.60m) [or 0.5mm in scale] high and about 75ft (23.5m) [or 19mm in scale] long, extending aft from a point about halfway along the forward funnel. Note that the central part of the front of the Navigating Bridge, in way of the screen windows, extends forward in a shallow curve.

Britannic as completed.

This shows the interesting new profile which *Britannic* introduces into the White Star fleet.   *Photographs: author's collection*

The lifeboats are stowed on deck, with a second boat superimposed where shown, all of which used quadrant davits. Hatches and cargo-handling gear are standard for the period, the winches being electrically driven. Electric cable holders were used for the anchor cables and there is a warping winch with extended arms immediately abaft the cable holders. A breakwater is set at an angle across the deck from the corners of the forward coaming to No 1 hatch. On the forecastle deck are a large number of mushroom-top ventilators, which are indicated by two concentric circles on the deck plan with their heights shown on the sectional profile. On the Boat Deck and elsewhere are a number of plenum ventilation units, which are indicted on the deck plans by small rectangles with a diagonal line. Although the units varied slightly in size, they can be represented by small blocks of wood about 40in high x 36in x 24in (1m x 0.8mm x 0.05mm), painted white. The funnels are oval, and both are plated over about 4ft (1.2m) below the top. The forward one is a dummy, but the top plate in the after one is pierced by a number of exhaust outlets. The tops of the funnels are level and parallel to the waterline.

Colour Scheme

Hull: black to the line of top of B Deck bulwarks, red below waterline; narrow yellow ribband at the level of B Deck.

Superstructure, deckhouses: white.

Lifeboats, davits: white; light grey covers.

Cable holders, winches, anchors, winches, bollards, fairleads, capstans: black

Hatches: dark grey.

Masts, derricks: mid brown.

Ventilators, skylights: white.

Decks: all wood planked.

Funnels: White Star buff, black tops. Note that White Star Buff has a very slight but distinctive touch of pink in it.

References

Motor Ship (mid-June 1930): illustrated technical article, with an external profile plan and some accommodation-only plans (no deck details). Most sources of ship photographs have shots of the ship, from before and after the war. There are references, in varying details to the ship in many books covering the Line's history, and liners in general.

Britannic (1930) White Star Line

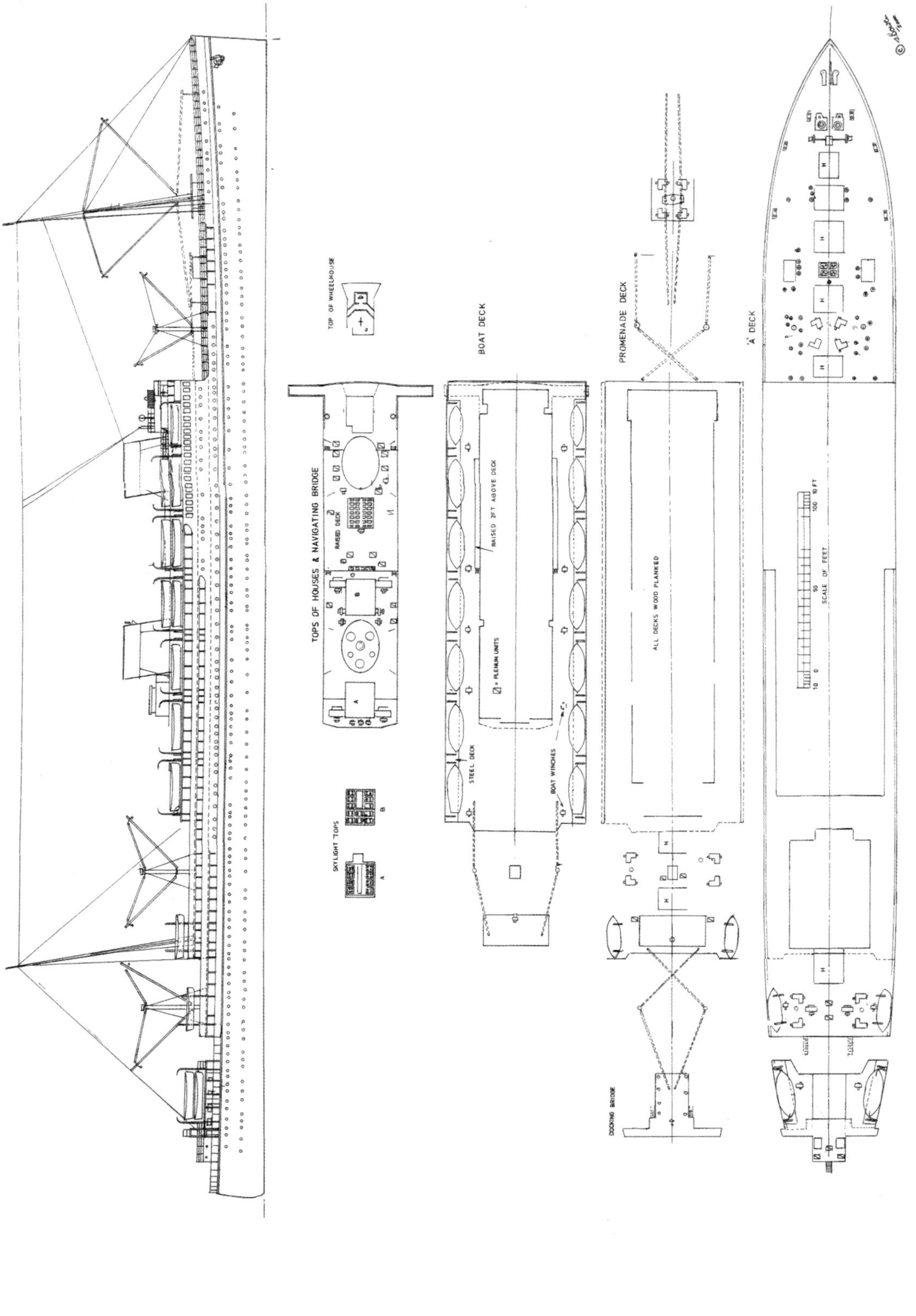

TOP OF WHEELHOUSE

TOPS OF HOUSES & NAVIGATING BRIDGE

RAISED DECK

SKYLIGHT TOPS

BOAT DECK

STEEL DECK

BOAT WINCHES

RAISED 2FT ABOVE DECK

2 = PLENUM UNITS

PROMENADE DECK

ALL DECKS WOOD PLANKED

DOCKING BRIDGE

'A' DECK

100 10 FT

50

SCALE OF FEET

10 0

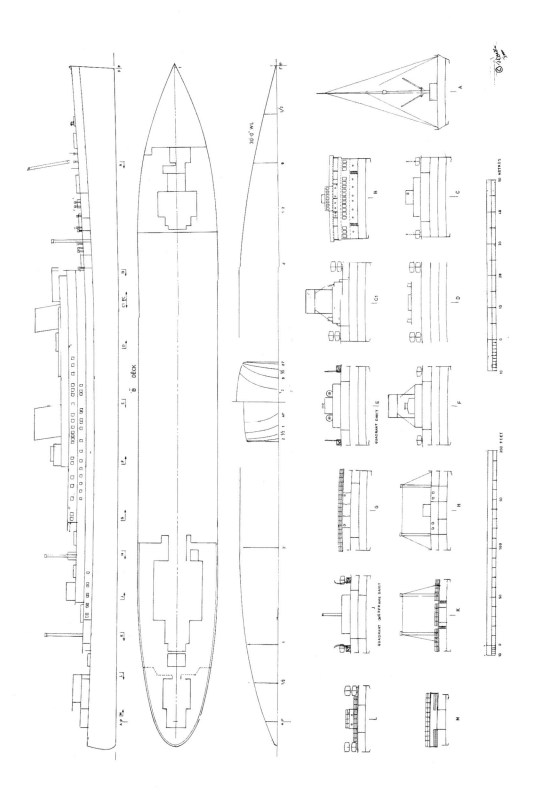

7

Calgarian
(1914)

ALLAN LINE

In 1911 the Allan Line, concerned at the success of the Canadian Pacific's 1906-built Empresses on the Canadian passenger trade, decided to build two new liners. The *Alsatian* and the *Calgarian*, as the new vessels were named, were extremely successful and considered by many to rank among the most attractive passenger ships of that era. The orders for both ships went to shipyards on the Clyde, the *Alsatian* being built by William Beardmore Ltd at Dalmuir, and the *Calgarian* by the Fairfield Shipbuilding & Engineering Co Ltd at Govan, Glasgow.

Although they were always referred to as sister-ships, and externally looked very alike, there were differences, as will be seen. Strongly built of steel, to improved standards of sub-division (being rated as 'four-compartment ships'), they were the first Atlantic liners to have a cruiser stern. The beam of the Fairfield ship was some 2ft less than that of the Beardmore vessel – 70.3ft against 72.4ft. No reason for this has been found.

The *Alsatian* was completed a few months ahead of her sister and left Liverpool on her maiden voyage to Canada on 17 January 1914. The *Calgarian* made her maiden voyage in May. Their employment on this service was to be of short duration. Within days of the outbreak of war in August 1914, the *Alsatian* was taken over by the Admiralty for service as an armed merchant cruiser and joined the 10th Cruiser Squadron patrolling off Shetland. Some months later she was given better guns and became the flagship of the Squadron upon the withdrawal of the old armoured cruisers, which were proving quite unsuitable for service in those stormy northern waters. In this role she served with distinction and on the disbandment of the squadron in 1917 she spent the remaining war years on Atlantic convoy work, being returned to her new owners at the end of hostilities. These new owners were the Canadian Pacific Railway Company, who had acquired the Allan Line in 1917.

Specification

Length bp:	570ft 0in (173.7m)
Breadth:	70ft 0in (21.3m)
Draught (approx):	28ft 0in (8.5m)
Tonnage, gross:	17515
Machinery:	steam turbines, 21,000shp; quadruple screw
Speed:	18 knots

At the beginning of 1919 they sent the ship back to her builders for a thorough refit to peacetime standards, and at the same time renamed her *Empress of France*. During the next twelve years she was employed mainly on the UK to Canada service, but by 1931, with the arrival of the new *Duchess* and *Mont* class ships, she was withdrawn and laid up. In 1934 she was sold to W H Arnott Young for scrap, being broken up in their yard at Dalmuir, very close to the berth from which she was launched 21 years earlier.

The *Calgarian* was also taken over by the Admiralty shortly after the outbreak of war for use as an armed merchant cruiser. After some months on blockade duty off neutral ports such as Lisbon and New York, she was diverted to escort duties with the North Atlantic convoys. She was not as fortunate as her sister. In March 1918 she was escorting an eastbound convoy to the Clyde, and had reached the vicinity of Rathlin Island off Fair Head, North Antrim, Northern Ireland, when she was struck by four torpedoes and sank very quickly with the loss of 49 of her crew.

There were some external differences between the two ships. Apart from a variation in the spacing of the Promenade Deck windows below the bridge, the *Calgarian*

Calgarian

Photograph from Keeper of the Records of Scotland

can always be identified by two other features: the short length of side plating below the Promenade Deck forward and the omission of the arched curtain plate between the Boat Deck stanchions. This latter feature could be a problem on the small-scale model of the *Alsatian*, for unless it is done absolutely uniformly and to scale, the whole appearance and character of the model would be ruined.

Modelling Notes

The hull block can be taken up to the level of the Bridge Deck and then cut away at the after end down to the level of the Shelter Deck. The between-deck height of the houses on the Shelter, Bridge and Promenade Decks is 8ft 6in (2.65m). On the Boat Deck there are areas of raised deck 2ft 6in (0.75m) high in way of the bridge, under the dome and house lying between the funnels, under the funnels and under the deckhouse abaft the after funnel. The houses on

top of the raised deck areas are 8ft (2.5m) high, but the dome is only 6ft (1.8m) high at the centre.

There are 18 lifeboats, carried under radial davits fitted outside the deck edge curtain plate, the heels of the davits being level with the bottom of the Promenade Deck bulwark. An Englehart collapsible lifeboat is stowed beneath each lifeboat, except in way of the aftermost lifeboat on each side where two such boats are stowed. In addition two Englehart boats are stowed port and starboard inboard on the Boat Deck abreast the forward funnel, and a further two boats are stowed each side inboard of the aftermost lifeboat.

The ten steam winches for handling the cargo are of the normal standard pattern. There are six capstans, two on the Bridge Deck forward and four on the Shelter Deck aft. Cable holders are used to handle the anchors. Note the shape of the breakwater built on to the fore end of the fore-

Calgarian (1914) Allan Line

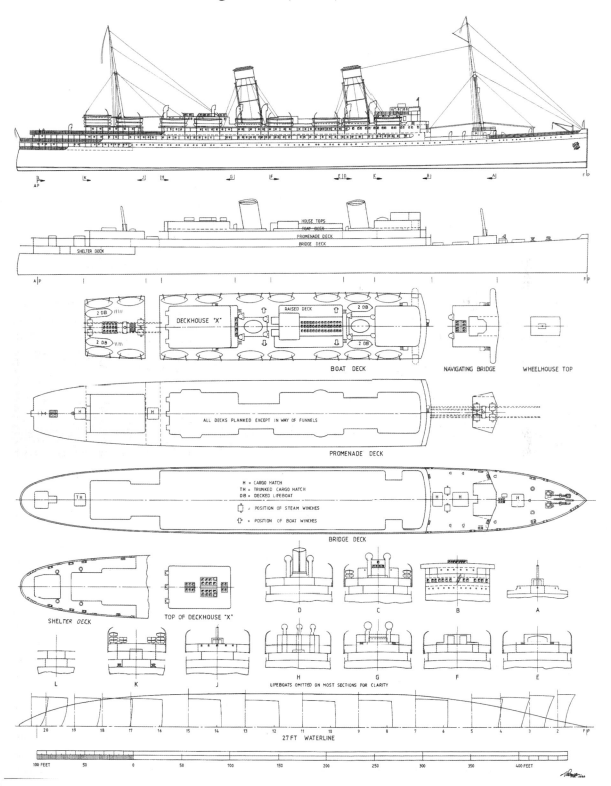

most deckhouse (see section A). The funnels are elliptical in section and are surmounted by a prominent cowl top (for method of construction see entry for funnels in Part 1, p25).

Colour Scheme

Hull: black to the level of the top of the Shelter Deck bulwark, white above to the level of the Bridge Deck; boot topping red, separated from the black by a narrow white ribband.

Superstructure, deckhouses: white.

Wheelhouse: front white, sides and after end mahogany.

Inside bulwarks: white.

Lifeboats: white, natural canvas covers, gunwale brown; Englehart boats white.

Davits: white.

Ventilators: white, inside of cowls red.

Masts and derricks: golden brown.

Winches: black.

Bollards, fairleads: black.

Cable holders, anchors, capstans: black.

Funnels: red, broad white band below black top section.

Deck: all planked, but black steel deck in way of funnels.

References

Ravenscraig, The Allan Royal Mail Line by Thomas E Appleton (Toronto: McLelland & Stewart Ltd, 1974) is the definitive history of the Allan Line; *The Big Blockade* by E Keble Chatterton (London: Hurst & Blackett, 1932) is the story of the work of the 10th Cruiser Squadron and of the part played by the *Alsatian*; *North Atlantic Seaway* by NPR Bonsor (first published by T Stephens & Sons, Ltd in 1955 and a completely revised edition published by David & Charles in 1975) contains a chapter on the Allan Line (in both editions); 'Allen Liners *Alsatian* and *Calgarian*' by JH Isherwood in *Sea Breezes* Vol 23 (April 1957).

Articles on and general arrangement (GA) plans of the *Alsatian*: *Shipbuilder & Marine Engine-Builder* (February 1914); *Engineering* (4 April 1913 and 26 December 1914).

Glasgow City Archives (see Appendix II, pp205–206) have plans of most of the ships built at Fairfield (the National Maritime Museum, Greenwich, has some of the earlier vessels) including: ½in = 1ft scale GA plan of *Calgarian* – ref no UCS2/120/487/12; ¼in=1ft scale lines and body plan – ref. no UCS2/132/487/59; and one photograph of *Calgarian*, probably running trials – ref no UCS2/132/487/1.

8

Californian
(1902)

LEYLAND LINE

The *Californian*, along with the Cunard liner *Carpathia*, is a ship irrevocably associated with the *Titanic* disaster. The *Californian* was built in 1902 by the Caledon Shipbuilding Company Ltd, Dundee, Scotland (Yard No 159) for the Leyland Line's (Frederick Leyland & Co Ltd) North Atlantic service. With her four masts, single funnel and flush deck hull, she was a typical cargo ship of the period. She was also given a certificate to carry 47 passengers. A single-screw vessel, the triple expansion machinery gave her a speed of 13.5 knots.

Apart from the connection with the *Titanic* disaster, she was just a hard-working unit of the owner's fleet, and continued to serve in that capacity until she was torpedoed and sunk off Cape Matapan on 9 November 1915.

Specification	
Length overall:	464ft 0in (141.4m)
Length bp:	447ft 6in (136.4m)
Breadth mld:	53ft 6in (16.3m)
Draught:	27ft 0in (8.3m)
Tonnage, gross:	6223 tons
Machinery:	triple expansion, single screw
Speed:	13.5 knots
Passengers:	47

Sources

The Caledon yard closed in 1981 and all surviving plans from this company are held at the City of Dundee District Archives. When I contacted them it transpired that they had only one plan for the *Californian*, which turned out to be a very simple small-scale sectional profile and general arrangement of the Shelter and Promenade Decks. Only essential details were shown. In addition they had two photographs: one bow view of the ship ready for launching and one onboard deck taken from a viewpoint on the port side of the Shelter Deck aft, abreast the jigger (aftermost) mast looking forward. There are references to the ship and her role in the *Titanic* disaster, together with a couple of bad-quality photographs (not the fault of the authors or publishers, just the conditions under which they were taken) in the books listed under references at the end. Other photographs of the ship appear to be very difficult to locate. There is one, taken later in her life, which shows that a small deckhouse had been added at the after end of the Promenade Deck between the engine room skylight and the end of the deck.

Modelling Notes

The hull is flush decked, with a somewhat flat sheer, a straight and almost vertical stem and a typical counter stern. The flare on the bow is not too pronounced, as can be seen on the body plan. Although the superstructure extends out to the ship's side, it will be found easier to carve the hull to the level of the Shelter Deck and add the midships house as a separate piece.

The Shelter Deck is planked throughout forward and aft of the midship house. However, in way of Nos 2 and 6 hatches there is an area of deck each side between the hatch coamings and the ship's side which is covered with what are best described as standard-type wood hatch covers laid fore and aft, with their top surface level with the top of the deck planking. On each side of the hull, in way of these areas, there is a pair of hinged doors extending from the Shelter Deck to the deck below. These are shown on the elevation of the plan as rectangles, but would not be visible on the black hull of a model.

The two derricks on the after side of the foremast, mizzen

mast and jigger mast stow in a line one above the other, as shown on the plan. Elsewhere, where there are two derricks on a mast they stow side by side. The single derrick on the after side of the mainmast is stowed vertically against the mast. A single steam winch serves each hatch, except on No 3 where there are two, one forward and one aft of the hatch.

On the Promenade Deck the lifeboats are stowed on Y-shaped pedestals, with the keel level with the top of the guardrails (i.e. about 3ft 6in [1.07m] above the deck). The boats are handled by standard radial-type davits set in pedestals on the deck. This deck is wood planked, but the top of the boiler casing is bare steel. The small rectangle at the forward end of this casing, between the ventilators, is a fiddly grating.

Colour Scheme

Hull: black, red-brown below the waterline; narrow yellow ribband round the hull with the top edge about 2ft (0.6m) below the edge of the Shelter Deck.

Superstructure: white; lower half of side of midship house black (i.e. to level of top of Shelter Deck guard rails); lower half of forward and after ends of the midship house, and the sides and ends of deckhouse at the after end of Shelter Deck, mid-brown; houses on Promenade Deck white; engine room skylight white, but the casing on which it is fitted is mid-brown.

Ventilators: black, inside cowls white.

Lifeboats: white, light grey canvas covers; davits and pedestals white.

Hatches: black, tops grey.

Windlass, winches: black.

Masts, derricks: brown.

Funnel: pink, black top. The pink colour is the same shade as that of the Bibby Line funnels, the nearest Humbrol colour being No 61, Flesh.

Water tanks, etc: white.

References

Sea Breezes Volume 16 'Sixty Years of the Leyland Line'; *The Ship That Stood Still* by Leslie Reade, edited by Edward P de Groot (New York: W W Norton 7 Co, 1993); *The Titanic and the Californian* by Peter Padfield (Hodder & Stoughton, 1965); *The Titanic Myth – The Californian Incident* by William Kimber (The Self-Publishing Association, 1986, updated 1992); *Titanic - Triumph & Tragedy* by John P Eaton & Charles H Haas (Patrick Stephens, 1986); City of Dundee District Council Archives house the small-scale GA plan and two photographs mentioned above.

The *Californian*: this photograph would seem to have been taken later in her life, as what appears to be a small deckhouse has been added at the after end of the Promenade Deck between the end of the deck and the after end of the engine room skylight.

Photograph: author's collection; original source unknown

Californian (1902) Leyland Line

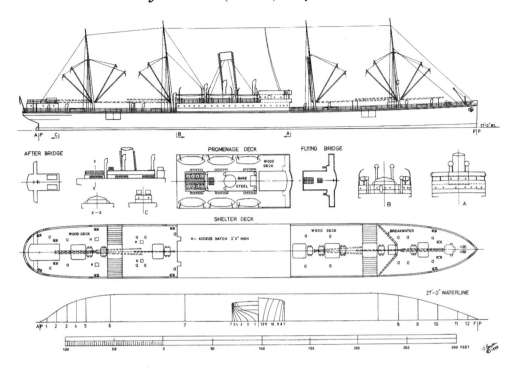

9

Capetown Castle
(1938)

UNION-CASTLE MAIL STEAMSHIP CO LTD

Following the success of the liners *Stirling Castle* and *Athlone Castle*, whose speed enabled the voyage between Southampton and Cape Town to be made in under two weeks, and major alterations to five more of their liners to meet the requirements of the mail contract on the same route, the Union-Castle Mail Steamship Company placed an order with Harland & Wolff Ltd, Belfast, for an eighth ship for the service. This was the *Capetown Castle* (Yard No 986). She was launched on 23 September 1937, delivered at the end of March 1938 and sailed on her maiden voyage on 29 April 1938. Although very similar in appearance to *Stirling Castle* and *Athlone Castle* she was larger and more powerful, and in fact at that time was one of the largest motor ships in the world. I have always felt that she was the best looking of all the post mid-1930s Union-Castle liners. The *Edinburgh Castle* of 1948 was the most like the Capetown as completed, but was spoiled by the rather large and more upright funnel; later alterations did not improve matters.

Capetown Castle was taken up for trooping duties when war broke out in September 1939 and continued to serve in that role until handed back to her owners in 1946. After a thorough overhaul by her builders she returned to the South African service in January 1947 and continued on that run until 1967 when she was withdrawn and sold, being broken up at La Spezia, Italy.

Modelling Notes

The hull should be made to the level of D Deck. When shaping the hull note that it has a good flare forward and that the cruiser stern is fairly full bodied. It is important to get the correct curve to the stem. The bow bulwark, from aft of the opening in way of the fairlead, has a pronounced knuckle at deck level. It can be made from a piece of mounted shaving (with the grain running vertically), glued to the

Specification	
Length overall:	734ft 3in (223.8m)
Length bp:	685ft 5in (206.9m)
Breadth mld:	82ft 0in (25.9m)
Draught:	32ft 0in (9.6m)
Tonnage, gross:	27,000 tons
Machinery:	2 x 10 cyl Harland-B & W diesels = 28,000 bhp; twin screw
Speed:	20 knots
Passengers (as built):	292 first class, 499 cabin

edge of the deck, but great care will have to be taken to make sure that it follows the curve of the stem and flare of the bow forward of that fairlead opening. The expanded shape of the bulwark can be obtained by placing a strip of mounted shaving (paper side inboard) round the bow, with the top edge about 5mm above the deck line, and pinching it in firmly against the hull with thumb and forefinger. Run a sharp pencil round the inside at deck level, mark the position of the centre line on the paper and also the position of the after end of the bulwark each side, which should have been marked on the deck beforehand. That done, the mounted shaving should be flattened out and a line drawn parallel to, and to the height of the bulwark above, the line of the deck. Carefully cut out the bulwark and glue in place. It is better to trim the curved ends of the bulwark once it is in place; this can be done with the tip of an unused (new) fine-pointed Swann Morton blade.

Alternatively, a piece of lime (of a thickness equal to the

height of the bulwark and width of the hull block) can be glued to the hull block after the sheer has been cut and finished, but before the sides of the block are carved to shape. The centre part of this piece should be cut away to within about 2mm of the edge of the deck before fitting. Once the bow has been carved, the flare formed and the outside of the bulwark carved to its more upright configuration, and with the pronounced knuckle at deck level formed, the inside must be very carefully pared away until a wafer thin bulwark is formed. The ends should be trimmed to shape in the way described above.

The opening in each side of the hull forward in way of the Upper (C) Deck can be cut out with a narrow chisel down to the level of B Deck, leaving a thickness equal to the depth of the curtain plate at the top. In reality this is an open area right across the ship from side to side and reaching fore and aft for a length slightly more than that of the openings in way in the sides of the ship. If included then the fore deck from bow to the front of the superstructure should be covered with a deck card. As this open area would hardly be visible unless carefully sighted through the two hull openings, a shallow opening each side about 4mm deep would suffice. Before fitting the bulwark, by the recess method, the interi-

or must be painted white. The deck stanchions can be made from very fine wire or plastic rod.

The way in which the various components of the superstructure are made and fitted follows the usual methods. However, the areas of curved plating around the front of the superstructure may present some problems and it is recommended that these be made in three main sections. The first section covers the front of the house on the Bridge (D) Deck, and must be cut to include the bulwark; provision will have to be made for the projection housing the two stairs. The front of this will have to be covered with a separate piece. The second section, covering the front of the house on the Promenade (E) Deck, and including the bulwark round the front of the Boat Deck, will have to be carried aft each side of the ship to include the large rectangular windows, and also the short length of bulwark which ends roughly in line with the after trackway of the second boat. Again, provision will have to be made for the projection housing the two stairs. The third section covers the front of the house on the Boat (F) deck, its bulwark and also the front of the wheelhouse and the bulwark round the Navigating Bridge wings.

It is essential that the windows are reproduced to an

Capetown Castle as she was following the postwar refit; note the white masts.   *Photograph: author's collection*

absolutely uniform size and are correctly aligned and spaced. One method of doing this is to make a drawing of this area several times larger than the finished scale size, and to reduce it to scale size on a photocopier. The degree of enlargement will be governed by the type of machine available, so before starting work it is advisable to check if the machine reduces/enlarges in single unit increments or only to three or four fixed ratios. If you can only reduce/enlarge to fixed ratios then the degree of enlargement must be worked out in relation to these ratios, so that the final reduction will give a drawing at 1/1200 scale. Take the piece for the front of the Promenade Deck as an example of drawing to a larger scale (it is assumed that at this stage the deckhouses and deck cards are in place). Put a mark on the Promenade Deck each side where the short bulwarks end and then measure the distance (girth) from one side point to the other. On a sheet of paper draw two parallel lines, one being the line of the Promenade Deck and the other the top of the bulwark on the Boat Deck. Mark off the girthed length just measured, then draw in the windows and the two short lengths of bulwark. Place a sheet of tracing paper or draughting film (used because it gives a cleaner, sharper copy) over the drawing, carefully trace the outline and put in all the windows and black in these rectangles. Have several copies made from the tracing.

The next step is to trim one of these copies to the deck and top of the bulwark lines, leaving a tail at each end to facilitate handling. Try it in place and make any alterations necessary to ensure a perfect fit, then cut out a second copy, incorporating any changes made to the first (which should be kept as a master template). Before cutting out the second give it a coat of clear matt varnish. When dry, glue in place, trim off the 'tails', and shape the end of the bulwarks. The piece for the front of the Boat Deck and Navigating Bridge can be prepared in a similar way.

There are a few points to notice about the fittings. The davit trackways are not radiused at the outboard end where they turn down to the deck, but meet the vertical piece at an angle. Note the prominent triangular brackets securing the track to the deck. This vertical piece is longer on the davits carrying the motor launches than on the other trackways. In most cases the inboard end of the trackway rests on the top of the adjacent deckhouse. For clarity, the boats and their cradles have been omitted on the cross sections of the plan.

The funnel is plated over below the rim, and a number of exhaust outlets of different diameters pass through the plating.

Colour Scheme

Hull: Union-Castle lavender grey to the level of the top of the bulwark to the opening in the ship's side forward in way of the Upper (C) Deck, white above, with narrow teak colour dividing line between; red below waterline (the nearest shade to this hull colour being obtained by mixing 10 parts Humbrol No 147 light Grey, 1 part Humbrol No 174 Signal Red, and 2 parts Humbrol No 104 Blue).

Superstructure: white, inside bulwarks white.

Masts, derrick posts, derricks: as built, masts were reddish-brown, derrick posts and derricks white. After the war the masts were changed to white.

Ventilators: white, inside cowls red.

Lifeboats, davits: white, boat covers light grey.

Windlass, winches: mid-grey.

Bollards, fairleads: black.

Hatches: grey.

Funnel: vermilion (orange red), black top.

Decks: wood planked, bare steel decks mid-grey

References

The articles in the following journals, apart from a technical description of the ship, only contain some outline deck and accommodation plans (none of the top decks) and an outline sectional profile: *The Motor Ship* (October 1937 and May 1838); *Shipbuilding & Shipping Record* (28 April 1938 and 30 December 1938).

For general reading about the company and its ships: *The Cape Run* by W H Mitchell & L A Sawyer (Lavenham, Suffolk: Terence Dalton, 1984); *Mailships of the Union-Castle Line* by C J Harris & Brian D Ingpen (Patrick Stephens Ltd, 1994).

The Ulster Folk & Transport Museum has a number of photographs of the ship under construction and running trials (in the Harland & Wolff Archive Photographic collection). Southampton City Council also has a number of photographs of the ship taken either in the docks or at sea. See Appendix II, pp205–206, for contact details.

Capetown Castle (1938) Union Line

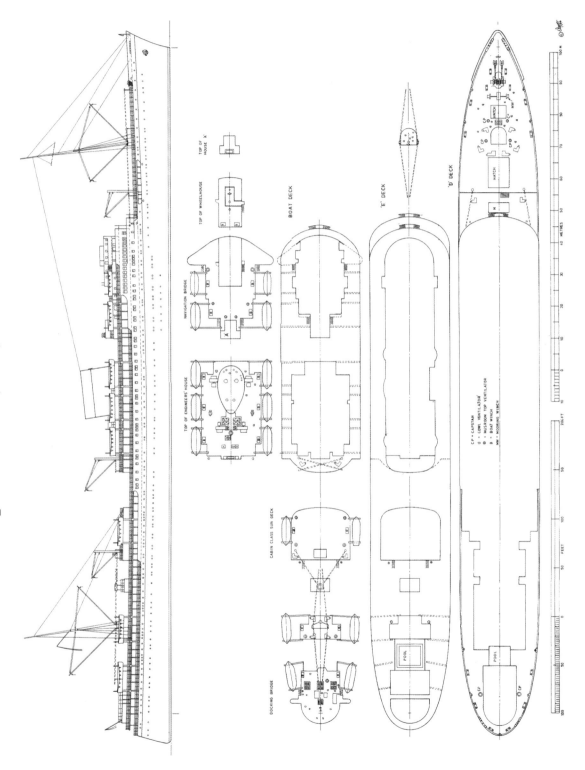

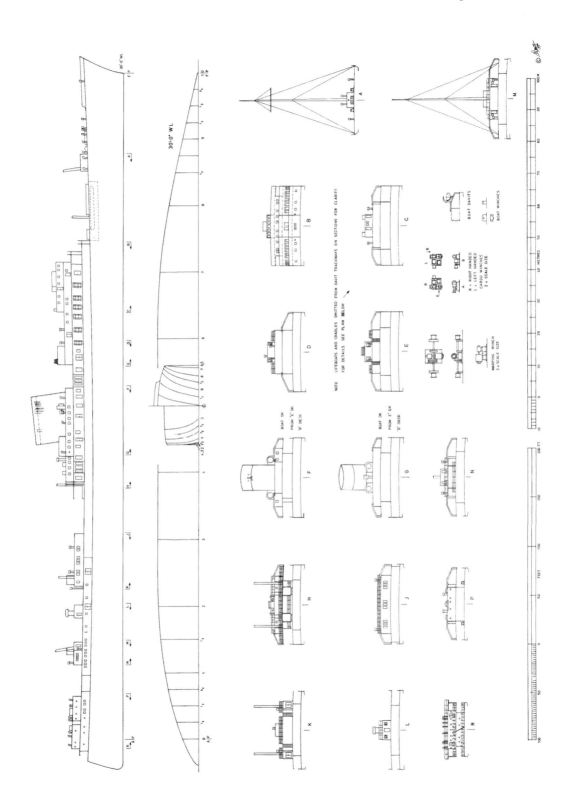

10

Carpathia (1903)

CUNARD STEAMSHIP COMPANY

The *Carpathia* was built in 1903 by C S Swan & Hunter at Wallsend-on-Tyne (Yard No 274) for the Cunard Company for their Liverpool to Boston service. However, within a year of making her maiden voyage to Boston she was moved to their Trieste to New York run where she remained for the next eleven years, with occasional transfers to the Liverpool to New York service as circumstances demanded.

She would have undoubtedly continued performing her tasks quietly and efficiently had she not picked up the White Star liner *Titanic*'s urgent distress call in the early hours of Monday 16 April 1912. The events that followed, and the splendid part played by the *Carpathia* and her crew – a role that immediately brought her into the full glare of publicity – have been fully recorded. Once the immediate aftermath of the loss of the *Titanic* had passed, *Carpathia* resumed her voyaging, and in 1915 was put on the Liverpool to New York run, carrying vital war supplies. But on 17 July 1918, whilst outward bound in convoy, she was torpedoed and sunk 170 miles north west of Bishop's Rock; five boiler room personnel were killed, but the remaining 275 crew and passengers were rescued.

Numerous models have been made of the *Titanic* but rarely is one seen of the *Carpathia*. Why this should be is unclear. She was a fine looking ship with a nicely balanced profile, typical of the intermediate liners on the North Atlantic in the early years of the twentieth century. Perhaps the answer to the question lies there: that she was just one of many; an ordinary intermediate liner? Or is it that very little information about the ship in the way of plans, as distinct from the activities, has appeared in print? The plan given here has been prepared from research that uncovered original and authentic material, and shows the ship as built.

Modelling Notes

The hull can be made in one of two ways. It can be carved to the level of the Bridge Deck and cut down to the level of the Shelter Deck at each end, or it can be made to the line of the Shelter Deck, with the long midship deckhouse added as a separate piece. In this latter case, the deckhouse piece can be made fractionally narrower than the finished width of the hull, so that a length of paper-backed shaving can be cut and glued along each side of the house and extended above deck level to form the bulwark running the length of the Bridge Deck level. This method has the added advantage of providing a clear, sharp dividing line that will act as a guide when applying the black and white paint to the hull and topsides. The rest of the work should present few problems. The cowl ventilators are a prominent feature of the profile. Note that some of the derricks are stowed vertically against their respective masts.

Colour Scheme

Hull: black above waterline, red below, with a narrow white dividing ribband.
Superstructure: white.

Specification

Length overall:	558ft 0in (170.08m)
Length bp:	540ft 0in (164.59m)
Breadth mld:	64ft 0in (19.51m)
Draught:	32ft 7in (9.93m)
Tonnage, gross:	13,555 tons
Machinery:	quadruple expansion, twin screw
Speed:	14 knots

The Cunard liner *Carpathia*   *Photograph: author's collection*

Masts and derricks: golden brown.

Windlass, winches, bollards, fairleads: black.

Boats and davits: white; boats have light grey covers without stabs.

Ventilators: white; inside cowls red.

Funnel: Cunard red, black top and three narrow black bands.

Hatches: coamings mast colour, top black.

Decks: wood sheathed, black steel in way of funnel.

References

The National Maritime Museum in Greenwich stores the Swan Hunter plan collection, sectional profile and general arrangement of decks (although the quality of these is not good, with loss of detail in several places); *Sea Breezes*, Volume 52 No 388 (April) contains an article by J H Isherwood in his 'Steamers of the Past' series.

Photographs: apart from the usual sources some photographs are reproduced in books dealing with the ships and history of the Cunard Line and books about the *Titanic*; among these latter books, *Titanic, Triumph & Tragedy* by John P Eaton & Charles A Hass (Wellington, Northants: Patrick Stephens, 1986) has a number of rare on-board scenes of *Carpathia* taken at the time of the rescue.

Carpathia (1903) Cunard Steamship Company

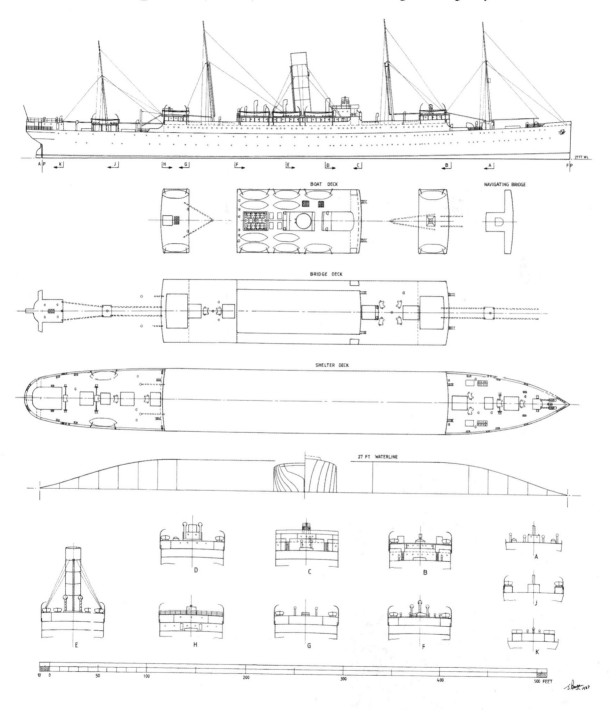

BOAT DECK   NAVIGATING BRIDGE

BRIDGE DECK

SHELTER DECK

27 FT WATERLINE

11

Clan Urquhart (1911/1933)

CLAN LINE STEAMERS LIMITED

In 1911 John Brown & Co Ltd of Clydebank built three very large ships for the Australia to UK meat trade, the *Argyllshire* (Yard No 399) for the Scottish Shire Line (Turnbull Martin & Co Ltd) and the *Shropshire* (Yard No 400) and *Wiltshire* (Yard No 401) for the Federal Steam Navigation Co Ltd. In 1933 *Argyllshire* was transferred to the Clan Line and renamed *Clan Urquhart*. She was broken up in 1936. *Shropshire* passed to the New Zealand Shipping Company in 1922 and was renamed *Rotorua*; she was torpedoed and sunk off the west coast of Scotland in December 1940. *Wiltshire* ran aground near Auckland, New Zealand, in May 1922 and became a total loss.

All three ships were imposing vessels, the long hull with a single funnel and five masts giving them a very distinctive

Specification

Length overall:	544ft 0in (165.8m)
Length bp:	525ft 0in (160.02m)
Breadth:	61ft 5in (18.71m)
Draught:	29ft 6in (9.02m)
Tonnage, gross:	10,393
Machinery:	quadruple expansion, twin screw
Speed:	13.5–14 knots

Clan Urquhart   *Photograph: A Duncan*

profile. Because they had to pass along the Manchester Ship Canal the top section of the funnel was removable, hence the presence of the narrow service platform round the funnel. The topmasts on all five masts were telescopic. Although the three ships were generally similar in external appearance, only *Shropshire* and *Wiltshire* were fitted with a prominent transverse platform between the two forward deckhouses.

Modelling Notes

The hull can be made to the line of the Sheer Deck. Note that there is an easy sweep to the sheer along the length of the hull. As the body plan shows, the flare of the bow is not very pronounced. The shape of the counter stern, as seen in profile, differs slightly from the form more usually seen. It is better to make and fit the two deckhouses right forward before working on the bow bulwark to provide it with a useful anchorage. The long bulwark each side amidships is better fitted by cutting a shallow rebate about ⅟₁₆in deep, and to the thickness of the paper mounted shaving from which each bulwark will be cut.

The rectangular deckhouses and the overhanging decks of the superstructure are quite straightforward to make and assemble, each being painted and having doors and windows/portholes added before being fitted in place. Note that the fore end of the long midship house on the Shelter Desk is square, whereas the end of the one on the Promenade Deck above extends beyond the end of the house and is slightly curved. All decks are wood sheathed but the funnel sits on a shallow raised casing, which is painted black. To facilitate the release of the top section of the funnel there is a narrow platform all round the funnel, with a single bar handrail, about 3ft (0. 9m) below the point of separation. As each of the five topmasts can be telescoped into its lower mast, the lower masts below the outriggers must have a noticeably greater diameter than the topmasts. The latter should be made of a much finer pin, and can be secured to the outriggers with a spot of superglue.

Colour Scheme

Hull: black above waterline, red below.
Superstructure: white, inside of bulwarks white.
Deckhouses: white, tops of mast houses black.
Lifeboats and davits: white, boat covers mid grey.
Mast, derricks: mid grey.
Hatches: coamings mid grey, tops black.

The sister ship *Shropshire*, showing the prominent transverse platform fitted between the two forward deckhouses.

Photograph: J Byass

Clan Urquhart (1933) Clan Line Steamers Limited

Clan Urquhart sailing down the Clyde. This photograph was taken sometime in 1935–36, not long before she was broken up.

Photograph: John Bowen

Ventilators: mid grey, inside of cowls red.
Windlass, winches: black.
Bollards and fairleads: black.
Funnel: black, with two red bands separated by a narrow black band.
Decks: wood planked.

The two Federal ships had black topsides, red below the waterline with a narrow white dividing ribband; masts and derricks red/brown (Humbrol 73 and 100 mixed in equal parts); ventilators white with red on the inside of the cowls; funnel red with black top and company's logo each side (a white rectangle with a small blue rectangle in the centre of a red cross). As Argyllshire the hull was black, red below the waterline, with a narrow white dividing ribband; masts and

derricks red/brown; ventilators by funnel buff, remainder white; inside of all cowls red; funnel buff.

References

Some of the shipbuilder's plans for *Argyllshire* have survived; these include 339/1 Main and Upper Decks, 399/2 Shelter and Promenade Decks, 339/3 Boat Decks, Navigation Bridge and Rigging, 399/4 Profile and Hold, 399/5 Mid Section, 3997 Lines. Details can be obtained from the Glasgow University Business Record Centre (see Appendix II, pp205–206). It appears that no plans have survived for the two sister ships. The Scottish Record Office in Edinburgh has a number of good photographs of all three ships taken either when leaving the builder's yard or when on trials.

12

Corinthic (1947)

SHAW SAVILL & ALBION CO LTD

The *Corinthic* was one of four similar passenger–cargo steamers ordered by Shaw Savill & Albion Co Ltd just after the war for their UK to Australia and New Zealand service. *Corinthic* was constructed by Cammell Laird & Co in Birkenhead (Yard No 1759), while her sister ship *Athenic* (Yard No 1326) was built by Harland & Wolff Ltd, Belfast. The beam on the third and fourth of the steamers was increased by 1ft to 72ft. Of these, the *Ceramic* was also built by Cammell Laird (Yard No 1185) while the *Gothic* was constructed by Swan, Hunter & Wigham Richardson Ltd, at Wallsend on Tyne. *Corinthic* and *Athenic* were completed in 1947 with the second pair following a year later. All four vessels entered the owner's London to New Zealand service on completion.

They were fine, good looking ships, with a well-balanced profile. In addition to accommodation for 85 first-class passengers they had a good capacity for general and refrig-

erated cargo. *Corinthic* appears to have had an uneventful life. The passenger accommodation was removed in 1965, and thereafter she ran as a cargo ship. She was broken up at Kaohsiung in 1969. Of her sister ships, *Athenic* had the passenger accommodation removed in 1965, and she, too, was broken up at Kaohsiung in 1969. *Gothic* was fitted out as a Royal Yacht in 1951, but the proposed voyage did not take place. She was again fitted out as a Royal Yacht in 1953 for a voyage to Australia. It was at this time that the funnel was increased in height and fitted with a Thornycroft cowl. In 1968 she suffered a disastrous fire in the superstructure shortly after sailing from New Zealand. Following temporary repairs in New Zealand she returned to Liverpool. She was broken up at Kaohsiung in 1969. *Ceramic* was broken up at Tamise, Belgium in 1972.

Modelling Notes

The plans are of the ship as built. The hull can be made either to the level of the Shelter Deck, with the forecastle, bridge (midship house) and poop added as separate pieces, or can be cut to the level of the forecastle, bridge and poop decks and have the wells forward and aft cut out to the level of the Shelter Deck. The stem is raked, the bow has a nice easy flare and the cruiser stern is fairly full bodied. The sheer, about 12ft (3.7m) forward and 5ft (1.5m) aft above the height of deck amidships, gives a nice sweeping line to the top of the hull. The well decks forward and aft are protected each side by guard rails, with the side plating at the break of the forecastle and the poop, and at each end of the midship house, ending in the customary curve down to the deck, as shown on the plan.

The superstructure is made up of a number of more or less rectangular houses. The erections on the Shelter Deck, i.e. the forecastle, midship house and poop, are 8ft (2.44m) high. The houses on the Bridge and Promenade Decks are

Specification

Length overall:	560ft 0in (176.7m)
Length bp:	530ft 0in (161.5m)
Breadth mld:	71ft 0in (21.6m)
Draught:	29ft 7in (9.0m)
Tonnage:	15,237 tons gross, 11,365 tons deadweight
Displacement, full load:	22,350 tons
Machinery:	steam turbines 14,000 shp; twin screw
Speed:	17 knots
Passengers:	85 first class only

8ft 6in (2.6m) high, while those on the Boat Deck and on the Poop Deck are 8ft (2.5m) high. As the curtain plates, where fitted, would be at least 12in (0.3m) deep, the thickness of the material being used for the houses must be reduced by this amount if deck cards are being cut from scale 12in material to represent the curtain plates. The large house on the Boat Deck has a narrow extension at the fore end and it would be easier to add this as a separate unit rather than forming it with the rest of the house. Similarly, at the after ends of this house, on each side, there is a slight increase in width over the last 13ft (4m); this should be added as a separate piece each side. There is a bulwark across the fore end of the Bridge Deck. The fore end of the Promenade Deck is plated in for the full height to the Boat Deck, and the paper used for this should be carried up to form the bulwark to the Navigating Bridge and the front to the wheelhouse. As the corners of these decks are angular, the short lengths of full-height plating at the fore end of the Promenade/Boat Decks, and the shorter plating below, can be added as separate pieces. There is a short length of full-height plating between the Promenade and Boat Decks aft, which is carried round and across the after end of these decks for a distance of 12ft (3.6m) each side.

Although derricks and cargo winches are provided for servicing the two hatches on the Boat Deck (one abaft the officers' house and one at the after end of the deck), the hatches are flush (i.e. no raised coamings) to provide a clear area for deck games. Some photographs show that later in her life two additional derrick posts were fitted forward of the funnel. This may well have been done when the passenger accommodation was removed.

The fittings follow the usual pattern of the period. The hatches were fitted with board covers overlaid with tarpaulins. The two large cowl ventilators forward of the funnel were a prominent feature of the ship, and care should be exercised in getting these right. The trunk is 6ft (1.8m) in diameter, and the cowl 9ft 6in (2.9m) in diameter. The two mushroom-top ventilators abaft the funnel are 3ft (0.9m) in diameter, with the tops 5ft 6in (1.7m) diameter. The top of the funnel was plated over 6ft (1.8m) below the top, with a number of exhausts and other outlets passing through to a height of about 2ft (0.6m). The derricks were stowed horizontally, most fore and aft, although those on the two derrick posts on top of the officers' house on the Navigating Bridge were stowed transversely, as were the two on the after side of the two derrick posts at the after end of the Boat Deck. The other derrick on each of these latter posts stowed fore and aft. The heavy-lift derrick on the foremast stowed

The *Corinthic* as completed.

Photograph: Shaw Savill Line

Corinthic (1947) Shaw Savill & Albion Co Ltd

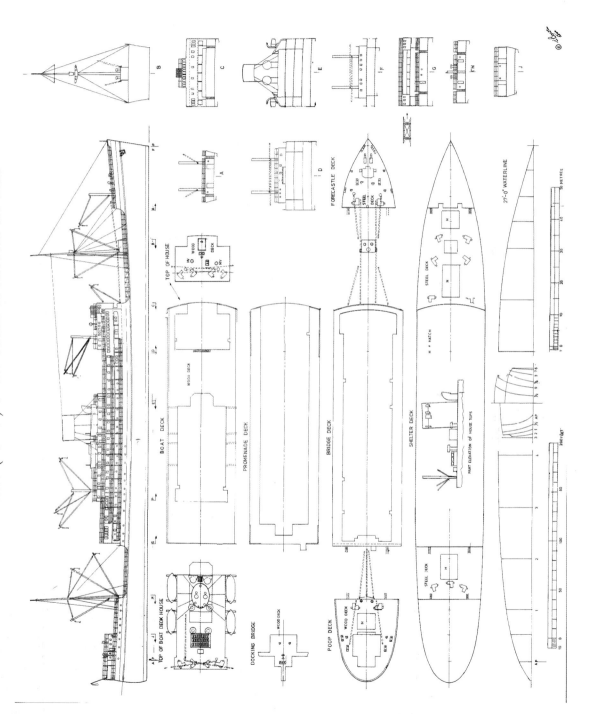

vertically on the after side of the mast. Full-height sliding glass screens closed off the open end of the verandah cafe at the after end of the midship house on the Promenade Deck.

Colour Scheme

Hull: black from waterline to a line 4ft (1.2m) above Shelter Deck; boot topping red; narrow yellow (gilt) ribband with the top edge at Shelter Deck level, and following the sheer of this deck.

Superstructure: white, break of forecastle, bridge and poop white; inside bulwarks white.

Hatches: dark grey.

Windlass, winches: dark grey.

Masts, derrick posts, derricks: deep buff (as funnel colour).

Ventilators: two cowl ventilators and two mushroom ventilators by the funnel, deep buff, as funnel; elsewhere white; inside of all cowls red.

Lifeboats and davits: white.

Funnel: deep buff, black top.

Decks: wood planked; forecastle deck bare steel, red oxide.

References

Illustrated technical articles, with photographs and small-scale arrangement plans (the profile is sectional not exterior) can be found in *The Shipbuilder & Marine Engine-Builder* (May 1947) and *Shipbuilding & Shipping Record* (1 May 1947). The Cammell Laird archives have the shipbuilder's lines, general arrangement of all decks, sectional profile drawings and a rigging plan.

Photographs: Skyfotos (see Appendix II, pp205–206) have several good aerial shots of *Corinthic* and her sister ships; most specialist vendors of ship photographs should have the ships in their lists.

For general reading about the company and its ships: *Shaw Savill & Albion* by Richard de Kerbrech (Conway Maritime Press, 1986), which deals with the post-World War II years; *Shaw Savill & Albion* by Duncan Hawes (TCL Publications, 1987), which is the 10th volume in the author's well-known Merchant Fleets series.

13

Derbyshire (1935)

BIBBY BROS

Derbyshire was built in 1935 by the Fairfield Shipbuilding & Engineering Co Ltd, Govan, Glasgow (Yard No 653) for the Bibby Bros' UK to Burma service. She was the last of the company's traditional four-masters. When Bibby Bros decided in the late 1880s to inaugurate a service between Liverpool and Rangoon and Colombo, they ordered two cargo ships (*Lancashire* and *Yorkshire*) from Harland & Wolff in Belfast, which were delivered in 1889. The vessels' four tall, raking masts, single funnel and vertical stem became the standard profile for subsequent new buildings, with two exceptions, ending with the *Derbyshire* of 1935. The exceptions were the *Dorsetshire* and *Somersetshire*, a pair of two-masted cargo ships ordered from Harland & Wolff in 1919 and handed over in 1920–21; from the outset they had been intended for later conversion to troopships, and this was done in 1927.

There was a certain stateliness about the Bibby four-masters, of which 19 were built over the years, although the five built between the wars, with their increased superstructures, perhaps lacked some of the elegance of the earlier vessels.

Derbyshire was converted to an AMC (Armed Merchant Cruiser) in 1940, but was decommissioned the following year and became a troopship, in which capacity she served until handed back to her owners in 1946. They sent her to her builders for a complete overhaul, which included major alterations to her profile, as can be seen in the photograph. She returned to the Burma service in 1947, and was broken up in the Far East in 1964.

Modelling Notes

A noticeable feature of the ship, though it does not apply to a waterline model unless it is being shown at the light load line, is the considerable curve to the forefoot, which starts at the load waterline. The hull should be carved to the level of the Poop, Bridge and Forecastle Decks, with the wells for-

Specification	
Length overall:	502ft 0in (153.00m)
Length bp:	482ft 0in (146.91m)
Breadth:	66ft 0in (20.12m)
Draught:	29ft 6in (8.99m)
Tonnage, gross:	11,650
Machinery:	2 x 8 cyl Sulzer Diesels, 8000 bhp; twin screw
Speed:	15 knots
Passengers:	291

ward and aft cut out down to the level of the Upper Deck. This should be carried out after the sheer has been cut but before any work is done to the sides of the hull. Once the hull has been shaped the bulwarks for the two well decks can be fitted. These should be cut from paper-mounted shavings and fitted by the rebate method.

As the plan shows, the various houses forming the superstructure, other than those on the poop, are rectangular. The 'tween deck height of the house on the Bridge Deck is 8ft 6in (2.6m), that on the Promenade Deck 9ft 6in (2.9m), but that of the separate house at the after end of that deck is 8ft 6in. The houses on the Boat Deck are 8ft 6in, but on the forward house on this deck the area on the plan shown with a hatched outline is 9in (0.23m) higher; which can be represented by a piece of thick paper glued on to the top of the house. The house on which the funnel is placed, on top of the Boat Deck house, is 6ft 6in (2.0m) high. The wheelhouse is 8ft high and there is a small platform at its after end, level with the top and supported by two light pillars, on which the standard compass is sited. It is surrounded by a teak bulwark 3ft 6in (1.0m) high.

On the superstructure there are open rails across the fore end of the Bridge and Boat Decks, but the fore end of the Promenade Deck is plated in, with the plating carried aft along each side as shown on the plan. Large rectangular windows are fitted in this plating. There is a bulwark across the front of the Navigating Bridge, between the wheelhouse and the bridge wing cabs.

The lifeboats are carried on gravity davits. The forward boat each side is a 22ft (6.71m) emergency boat. The second boat on the port side only is a motor launch. Note that on the Promenade Deck only there are double-deck stanchions below the davit trackways, reverting to a single stanchion on the deck below.

The children's play deck, on top of the house at the after end of the Promenade Deck, has a 5ft- (1.52m-) high safety railing (screen) all round with closely spaced uprights.

On the Upper Deck forward, in the well, there are two skittle alleys. Although no details are available about them, they probably comprised a long smooth track laid on top of the deck planking, as indicated on the plan, with vertical sides possibly about 12–18in (0.3–0.45m) high; in other words a flat-bottomed trough. The masts and the funnel all have the same rake of 8 degrees.

There is no raised surround to the swimming pool, the deck planking being carried out flush with the edge of the pool, finishing with a 12in- (0.3m-) wide margin plank round the pool. Access is by vertical metal ladders at the starboard side forward and the port side aft.

Colour Scheme

Hull: black, narrow gold ribband at the level of the top of the bulwarks to the Upper Deck in way of the wells forward and aft; salmon pink below waterline.

Superstructure: white; inside bulwarks white.

Masts, derrick posts, derricks: biscuit buff (nearest Humbrol colour is No 63 Sand).

Ventilators: white, inside cowls red.

Lifeboats, davits: white, light grey canvas covers.

Windlass, winches: light grey.

Bollards, fairleads: grey.

Hatches: light grey.

Funnel: 'Bibby' pink, black top. (the nearest Humbrol colour to 'Bibby' pink is No 61 Flesh).

Derbyshire as built.

Photograph: John Clarkson

Derbyshire (1935) Bibby Bros

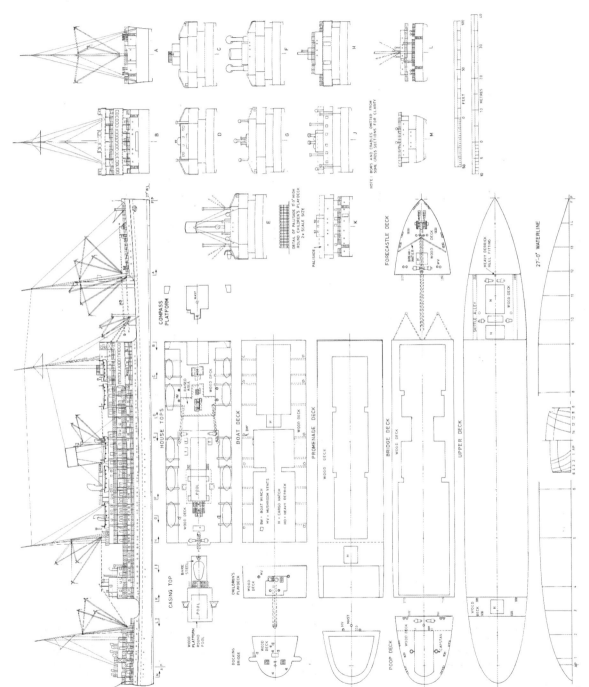

This shows the ship following the 1947 conversion: shorter, larger funnel, main and jigger masts removed, mizzen mast repositioned to become mainmast, pair of derrick posts fitted at break of poop, after end of superstructure shortened, well on upper deck aft extended forward and deckhouse added.

Photograph: author's collection

Decks: wood planked, bare steel decks red oxide.

Miscellaneous: water tanks, skylights white; anchor crane white; swimming pool light cream tiles with narrow blue line round sides and ends of pool 18in (0.45m) below top edge.

References

Illustrated articles with small-scale plans in *The Motor Ship* (November 1935) and *The Shipbuilder & Marine Engine-Builder* (January 1936); some 'as fitted' plans of the ship are held by Glasgow City Archives (see Appendix II, pp205–206).

For general reading about the company: *The Bibby Line 1807–1990* by Nigel Watson (Liverpool: Bibby Line Group Ltd, 1990 [ISBN 0-907383-12-3]); the Bibby Line company also published an earlier title *The History of the Bibby Line* by E W Paget-Tomlinson MA (1972); *The Burma Boats – Henderson & Bibby* by Duncan Haws (Duncan Haws, 1995 [ISBN 0-946378-26-6]) in the Merchant Fleets series.

14

Duchess of Bedford (1928)

CANADIAN PACIFIC

In the mid-1920s Canadian Pacific Steamships Ltd instituted a major building programme to replace some of the older vessels in their fleet. This included the construction of four large passenger ships for their Liverpool to Montreal service. Three of these, the *Duchess of Bedford*, *Duchess of Richmond* and *Duchess of York*, were ordered from John Brown & Co Ltd, Clydebank, Scotland (Yard Nos 518, 523 and 524 respectively). The order for the fourth ship, the *Duchess of Atholl*, was placed with Wm Beardmore & Co Ltd, Dalmuir (Yard No 648), whose shipyard was just a short way up river from Brown's yard.

The *Duchess of Bedford* was the first to be completed, making her maiden voyage to Montreal at the beginning of June 1928. With a nice sweeping sheer, well-balanced superstructure surmounted by two large funnels, all four were fine looking ships. At the beginning of World War II all of them were taken over by the government for trooping

Specification	
Length overall:	601ft 3in (183.26m)
Length bp:	580ft 0in (176.78m)
Breadth:	75ft 0in (22.86m)
Draught:	27ft 0in (8.22m)
Tonnage, gross:	20,500 (approx)
Machinery:	Single reduction geared turbines, 20,000 shp; twin screw
Speed:	17 knots
Passengers:	573 cabin class, 480 tourist, 518 third

The *Duchess of Bedford*

Photograph: author's collection

duties. *Atholl* was torpedoed and sunk off Ascension Island in October 1942 and *York* was lost by air attack in July 1943. The other two ships survived and were released back to their owners from government service in 1946–7. The vessels were sent to the Fairfield yard on the Clyde for complete overhaul and refurbishment to the standard of the company's *Empress* ships. Apart from very extensive alterations internally, the most noticeable structural difference externally was the enclosure of the whole of the Promenade Deck for the length of the Boat Deck above, and its extension aft to join up with the poop. The hull was repainted white, with green boot topping and a green ribband. The number of lifeboats was reduced and these became mahogany in colour. The company's red-and-white-chequered house flag was painted on each side of the funnels. The *Duchess of Bedford* was renamed *Empress of France* and the *Duchess of Richmond* became the *Empress of Canada*. Both ships returned to the Liverpool to Canada service. However, in 1953 the *Empress of Canada* was burnt out in

Liverpool and scrapped. Five years later, in 1958, the *France* was again overhauled and modernised, at which time she was fitted with new tall, tapered funnels with small, slanting cowls, which did not improve her appearance. But with the new *Empresses* (*of Britain, Canada* and *England*) now in service, she was withdrawn in 1960 and broken up at Newport, South Wales.

The plan shows her as completed in 1928, but one of the photographs shows her in the *Empress* livery.

Modelling Notes

The plans are for the ship as built. The hull can be carved to the level of the Bridge (B) Deck then cut down at the after end to the level of C Deck. When shaping the hull, note that the bow has quite an easy flare and that the cruiser stern is fairly full bodied.

There is a bulwark round the after end of C Deck, which is vertical above the line of C Deck and can be fitted by using a piece of mounted shaving or made integrally with

This photograph shows the *Duchess of Bedford* after her post-war overhaul and refit and renaming as the *Empress of France*.
Photograph: Canadian Pacific Photos

Duchess of Bedford (1928) Canadian Pacific

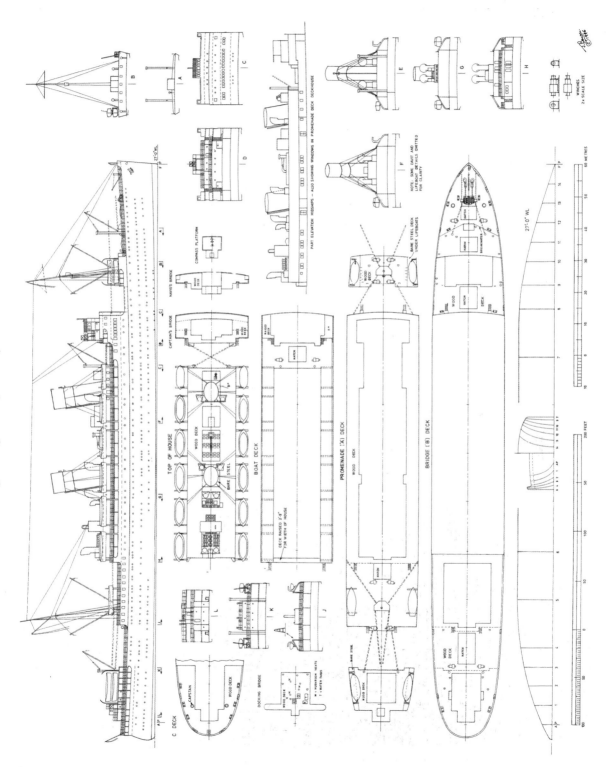

the hull (the method is given in the section on bulwarks in Part I – see p12). As this area will be covered by a deck card (B Deck) the deckhouse and any other fittings must be in place, painted and finished before the card is fitted. If the forward end of this card is carried forward as far as the after end of the house on this deck (i.e. roughly in line with a point just abaft the mainmast) the butt joint will be less visible. The top of the hull block in way of this card will have to be cut away by the thickness of the card being used.

On the superstructure the long bulwark each side on B Deck should be cut from mounted shaving and fitted either by cutting a shallow rebate along the side of the deckhouse, or by being glued on the edge of the house. As there is a sharp corner each side where the curved front of the superstructure meets the side of the superstructure, the paper used to cover the front and form the bulwarks can be made as a separate piece and does not need to be carried round and along each side to form the side screens, which can be cut as separate pieces.

The foremost and aftermost sets of lifeboats are stowed under quadrant davits, but the five sets of boats each side amidships comprise a 25ft (7.6m) boat stowed inside a 30ft (9.1m) boat, each being handled by gravity davits.

Colour scheme

Hull: black to level of C Deck; boot topping green.
Superstructure: white; wheelhouse, upper part of Navigating Bridge wing cabs above top of bulwark, wind deflector along top edge of bulwark across fore end of Navigating Bridge, mahogany (dark brown).
Masts, derrick posts, derricks: buff.
Ventilators: buff, inside cowls red.
Lifeboats, davits: white, light grey covers.
Windlass, winches: black.
Bollards, fairleads: black.
Hatches: buff.
Funnels: buff.
Decks: all wood planked.

References

The Shipbuilder (January 1929) contains a useful illustrated technical article, with small-scale general arrangement (GA) plans and midship section plan; Glasgow University Business Record Centre (see Appendix II, pp205–206) has the shipbuilder's Rigging, GA and a number of other plans for the ship, and also for the two sister ships (unfortunately none of Beardmore's plans have survived, but the four ships were virtually identical); *Sea Breezes* Vol 50 No 367 (July 1976) has an article on the ship in J H Isherwood's 'Steamers of the Past' series.

For general reading about the company: *Canadian Pacific* by George Musk (David & Charles, 1981 [ISBN 0-7153-7968-2]).

15

Empress of Ireland
(1906)

CANADIAN PACIFIC RAILWAY COMPANY

At the beginning of the last century the Canadian Pacific Railway Company, concerned at the dominance of the passenger and cargo trade between this country and Canada by the Allan Line, decided to order two new liners for this service. These were to be larger, faster and more luxurious than other vessels on the service. The order for the two ships was placed with the Fairfield Shipbuilding & Engineering Co Ltd, based at Govan in Glasgow, in 1904. The first of the pair, the *Empress of Britain* (Yard No 442), was completed in April 1906 and she was followed shortly afterwards by her sister ship, *Empress of Ireland* (Yard No 443). They were fine, well-proportioned ships with high freeboard, although some felt that the two funnels were a trifle on the thin side.

Both ships enjoyed great popularity from the time they entered the company's service between Liverpool and Canada, a service on which they ran without incident for several years.

However, this changed dramatically and tragically for the *Empress of Ireland* on 29 May 1914. Outward bound from Quebec to Liverpool in the early hours of that morning, she was proceeding cautiously in thick fog when she was in collision with the inward-bound Norwegian cargo ship *Storstad*. The Norwegian ship struck the *Empress* heavily on the starboard side almost amidships, inflicting such serious damage that she sank within 14 minutes, with a heavy loss of life. The details of the disaster and the ensuing public inquiry have no place here (though the *Empress* was subsequently cleared of all blame). These matters are well covered in two books, *Fourteen Minutes* by James Croall and *Forgotten Empress* by David Zeni (see References). The tremendous publicity that the tragedy attracted was heightened when it was learned that the master of the *Empress* was Captain Henry Kendall who, some years previously when in command of Canadian Pacific's *Montrose*, discovered that

Specification	
Length overall:	570ft 0in (173.74m)
Length bp:	550ft 0in (167.64m)
Breadth:	65ft 7in (19.98m)
Draught:	27ft 0in (8.23m)
Tonnage, gross:	14,191
Machinery:	quadruple expansion, 18,000ihp, twin screw
Speed:	18 knots

the wanted murderer Dr Crippen and his partner were among his passengers. The story of how he notified the authorities by wireless is also related in David Zeni's book.

In World War I the *Empress of Britain* served first as an armed merchant cruiser and then as a troop transport. When released from these duties at the end of the war, the Canadian Pacific Railway Company sent her up to her builders for a thorough overhaul and modernisation. In 1923–4 she was converted to a cabin-class ship and renamed *Montroyal*. She was sold to Norwegian shipbreakers in 1930.

Modelling Notes

The hull can be carved to the level of the Forecastle/Lower Promenade Deck, cutting down forward to the level of the Shelter Deck between the break of the forecastle and the midship house, and again at the after end to Shelter Deck level. Note that the hull has quite a marked tumblehome of 2ft (0.6m) each side at the Lower Promenade Deck level from the full beam of 65ft 7in at the waterline in way of the midships parallel body.

The *Empress of Ireland*: note that there is a very similar photograph of the *Empress of Britain*, which is often marked as being the *Empress of Ireland*; the easiest way to distinguish between the two, if the ship's name on the bow in not visible, is that on the *Britain* the space between the Lower and Upper Promenade Decks forward has been plated in over a length of about 50ft (15.0m) and houses seven rectangular windows.

Photograph: author's collection

On the superstructure, the house on the Upper Promenade Deck should be reduced in height to allow for the thickness of the card used for the deck, which will be equal to the depth of the deck's curtain plate. There are bulwarks along the sides and across the fore end of the Lower and Upper Promenade Decks and across the fore end of the Boat Deck. As shown on the plan, there is a central 2ft- (0.6m-) high raised area between the funnels on the Boat Deck. The deck each side under the boats is bare steel, with the remainder wood planked except for two small areas in way of the funnels.

The derricks are stowed horizontally, except for the pair on the fore side of the mainmast, which are stowed vertically against the mast.

The radial-type boat davits are fitted outside the edge of the Boat Deck, with the heel fittings at the bottom of the Upper Promenade Deck bulwark. The boats have canvas covers. There is a large capstan on the Forecastle Deck on the centerline and a windlass is fitted below the Forecastle Deck on the Shelter Deck to handle the anchors, which is why no hawse pipes are shown on the Forecastle Deck. Aft of the capstan is a breakwater, about 3ft (0.9m) high on the centreline, reducing to about 2ft (0.6m) high at the outboard ends. It is supported by brackets and the top is angled

forward; the outboard ends stop just short of the edge of the deck and they are finished with a radius. There are two compasses and a steering wheel on the top of the wheelhouse, along with two large cowl ventilators. The wireless office was situated in the house at the base of the mainmast, hence the unusual position of the aerial lead-in. The docking bridge is supported entirely on pillars.

Colour Scheme

Hull: black to the level of the top of the Shelter Deck bulwark, red below waterline, with a narrow white dividing ribband.

Superstructure: white.

Masts and derricks: buff.

Boats and davits: white, light grey canvas covers to boats.

Hatches: buff.

Winches, capstans: grey.

Bollards, fairleads: black.

Ventilators: large cowl ventilators on Boat Deck and top of wheelhouse buff, elsewhere white, inside of all cowls red; ventilation units white.

Funnels: buff.

Decks: all wood-planked, except for area under boats and two small areas in way of funnels which are black.

Empress of Ireland (1906) Canadian Pacific Railway Company

Miscellaneous: skylights, tanks, anchor crane white; fiddley gratings black.

References

Shipbuilder's plans for both ships, including rig, general arrangement of all decks, midship section and lines are held by the Glasgow City Archives (see Appendix II, pp205–206).

Engineering (20 July 1906, pp 95) contains an illustrated article (no plans) covering both ships; *Shipbuilding & Shipping Record* (13 March 1952) includes an article by Frank C Bowen [no relation to the author] on the *Empress of Britain*, which is No 163 in his series 'Ships that made history'; in *Sea Breezes* Volume 11 (February 1951) there is an article by J H Isherwood on *Empress of Britain* in his 'Steamers of the Past' series.

Fourteen Minutes – The Last Voyage of the Empress of Ireland by James Croall (Michael Joseph, 1978), which is also available in a 1980 paperback edition; *Forgotten Empress – The Empress of Ireland Story* by David Zeni (Tiverton, Devon: Halsgrove, 1998 [ISBN 1-874448-80-9]).

16

Felix Roussel
(1930)

MESSAGERIES MARITIMES

Every so often a ship or group of ships is built which, upon completion, arouses considerable interest. Such was the case when the first of the Messageries Maritime's three new motor liners, *Felix Roussel*, appeared in 1930. Intended for the company's Far Eastern Service, the *Felix Roussel* and her sisters, *Georges Philippar* and *Aramis*, introduced a standard of comfort and decoration hitherto unheard of on that route. But it was the two large, square, flat-topped funnels which evoked the most comment – complimentary and otherwise. Just why this should have been so is a little puzzling, since the Company's smaller motor liner *Eridan* of 1929 was fitted with two somewhat similar funnels.

The *Felix Roussel* was completed in 1930 by Ateliers et Chantiers de la Loire at Saint-Nazaire in France. After several generally uneventful years on her designated service, the *Felix Roussel* was withdrawn in 1935 and sent to a French shipyard for major engine modifications, which increased her speed by four knots. At the same time she was lengthened forward by 35ft (10.7m) by the addition of a semi-bulbous bow – its nicely raked stem replacing the original vertical one – and making a considerable improvement to her overall appearance. The hull, hitherto black, was painted white.

She remained on her former service until July 1940 when, following the fall of France, the British Sea Transport Office requisitioned her. For the next six years she was engaged in trooping and other duties, being returned to her owners early in 1946. She reverted to her original Far Eastern service and pre-war colours of black hull and black funnels. In 1948 she was withdrawn for a major overhaul and re-engining, which took two years; when she emerged her appearance was greatly changed. Gone were the two square funnels, replaced by a single oval funnel. The hull was now painted white, with green boot topping, and the funnel was

Specification

Length overall:	561ft 9in (171m)
Length bp:	535ft 0in (163m)
Breadth:	68ft 0in (26.7m)
Draught:	28ft 0in (8.5m)
Tonnage, gross:	15,000 tons
Machinery:	two 10-cylinder Sulzer diesel = 10,000bhp
Service speed:	14 knots

also white, as were the boats, superstructure, cranes, etc.

The introduction of new ships on the service and changing conditions in the Far East led Messageries Maritime to sell the ship in 1955 to the Swiss-owned Arosa Line. This company renamed her *Arosa Sun* and sent her to an Italian shipyard for overhaul and conversion to a tourist-class ship for service on the North Atlantic. During the next few years further modifications and alterations were carried out, and latterly she had a somewhat chequered career. In 1960 she was sold to a Dutch company for conversion to a floating hostel for workers at Ijmuiden. She served in this capacity for the next 13 years, except for a short spell in 1963 when she was under repair following severe damage by fire. In 1974 she was sold to Spanish shipbreakers and broken up at Bilbao.

Felix Roussel had a long and varied career in which she saw many changes, and outlived her two sister ships. *Aramis* was captured by the Japanese forces at Saigon in 1942 and torpedoed and sunk by an American submarine off the Philippines in 1944. *George Philippar*, it will be remembered, was destroyed by fire in May 1932 when off the Gulf

Felix Roussel as completed: note the straight stem and short forecastle.

Photograph: author's collection

of Aden on the return leg of her maiden voyage to the Far East, with the loss of many lives.

Modelling Notes

The main point to watch when carving the hull is the shape of the stern. The rather shallow counter is a feature of these three ships. It is better to make C Deck the top of the hull block and add the forecastle and long deckhouse to it, building up the rest of the superstructure in the usual way. The funnels are plated over at the top, level with the bottom of the overhanging top section. Except for the two in front of the bridge, which are slightly shorter, the crane jibs are all the same size and must be set at the same angle.

Colour Scheme

Hull: black from waterline to level of C deck, white above; boot topping green.
Superstructure: white; bulwark on Navigating Bridge brown.
Masts, derrick posts, derricks, cranes: white.
Lifeboats and davits: white.
Windlass, winches, bollards, etc: black.

Funnels: black.
Ventilators: white.
Decks: all planked.

References

The technical journal *The Motor Ship* (November 1930) contains an article with a GA plan (the profile is a sectional one, not an outboard elevation) of *Felix Roussel*; in another issue of the same journal (September 1932) a similar article appears on the *Aramis*.

Two very detailed articles about these ships, including an account of the loss of the *Georges Philippar*, and of the *Felix Roussel* under Arosa Line ownership, were published in *Steamboat Bill* No 144 (Winter 1977) and No 168 (Winter 1983), which is the journal of the Steamship Historical Society of America Inc; there are also two articles in *Sea Breezes* Volume 23 (January–June 1957) in the February and March issues of the same year.

A history of the company and details of all its ships can be found in *Messageries Maritimes* by Duncan Haws (Duncan Haws, 1999 [ISBN 0-9466378-377-1]), which is No 37 in his 'Merchant Fleets' series.

Felix Roussel (1930) Messageries Maritimes

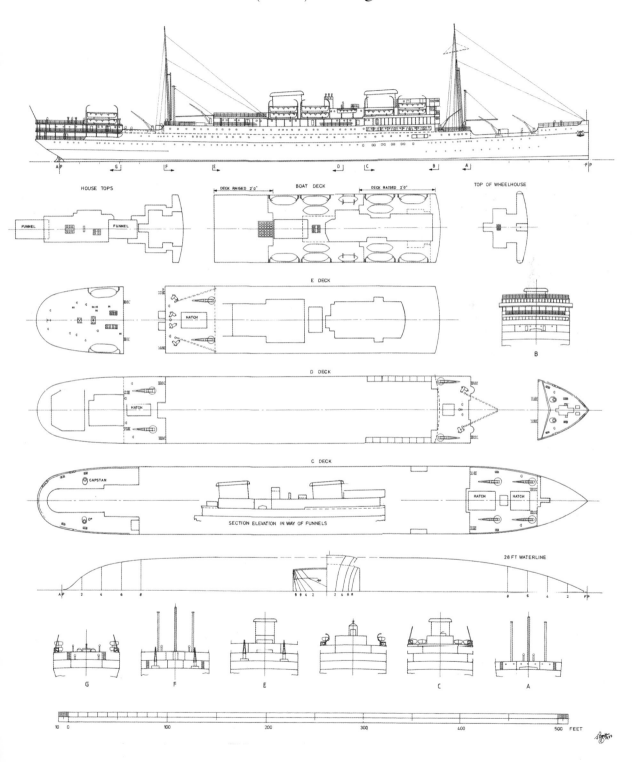

17

Glenogle
(1962)

GLEN LINE

*G*lenogle was one of the four fast cargo liners ordered by the Glen Line in 1960 for their UK to Far East service. She was constructed along with her sister ship *Glenfalloch* by the Fairfield Shipbuilding & Engineering Co Ltd, Govan, Glasgow. The *Glenlyon*, name ship of the class, was built by the Nederlandsche Dok en Scheepsbouw Maatschappij at Amsterdam, and the *Flintshire* by C Van der Giessen & Sons, Rotterdam. *Glenogle* was delivered in September 1962 with the others following in January 1963, October 1962 and December 1962 respectively. They were fitted to carry 12 passengers.

The Glen Line was a subsidiary of the Ocean Steamship Co Ltd, which was managed by Alfred Holt & Co (The Blue Funnel Line), and the *Glenlyon* class was designed by Ocean naval architects. While they bore a strong resemblance to Blue Funnel vessels, there were nevertheless some changes from traditional Holt practices. The flush deck,

with short forecastle and poop, was a departure from their customary three-island type, as was the grouping, for the first time, of all accommodation amidships. The fine lines and high engine power combined to give the required service speed of 20 knots, with enough reserve power in hand for 24 knots fully loaded should the need arise. Yet such was the changing pattern of the cargo-carrying trade that within a few years these very fine, advanced cargo carriers were to become outdated and uneconomic after comparatively few years of operation. *Glenogle* and her sister ship *Glenfalloch* passed to Chinese owners in 1978 and were still in service in 1991, bearing the names *Yang Chen* and *Qing He Cheng*. *Glenlyon* and *Flintshire* were acquired by Singapore owners in 1978 and renamed *Emerald Express* and *Orient Express* respectively. They were broken up in Kaohsiung in 1979.

Modelling Notes

The plan is of the ship as built. It can be used for the other three ships as well, subject to checking against photographs for any minor visible differences. The hull should be made to the level of the Upper Deck, with short prepared pieces added for the forecastle and the poop after the sheer has been cut but before the sides are shaped. The very fine lines of the hull forward, with the pronounced flare, well-rounded stem and hollow waterline are a marked feature of these vessels, and care must be taken to reproduce these as accurately as possible. The bulwarks, because they run from forecastle to poop, are better fitted by the rebate method. There is a recess in the bulwark each side, roughly amidships, in which an accommodation ladder is stowed. This makes it easier to fit the bulwark, as it can be made in three pieces: the first is from break of forecastle to the fore end of the recess; the second from the after end of the recess to the break of the poop; the third piece for the recess is glued to

Specification

Length overall:	543ft 9in (165.73m)
Length bp:	500ft 0in (152.40)
Breadth, mld:	74ft 6in (22.7m)
Draught:	30ft 0in (9.14m)
Tonnage:	11,916 tons gross 10,660 tons deadweight
Displacement:	19,040 tons
Machinery:	9-cyl Sulzer diesel, 16,600bhp (18,000 bhp max)
Speed (service):	20 knots
Passengers:	12

the deck, about 3ft (0.9m) in from the deck edge; it must have the ends turned at right angles to meet the shipside bulwarks. These are supported throughout their length by stays (brackets) spaced 5½ft (1.65m) apart.

On the Upper Deck and the Bridge Deck the screen or steelwork runs from the outboard corner of the fore end of the house on each of these decks to the ship's side, and then turns to run aft for a few feet – it is not, as is more customary, faired into the top of the bulwark plating but is kept just inside the bulwark rather than fastened to it, and extends from deck to deckhead with a narrow gap between it and the bulwark. This does make for much easier fitting on the model; in fact it could just be lapped against the inside of the bulwark.

The deck on the top of each of the four mast houses is supported by pillars at the corners; on the forward and aftermost houses there is one pillar at each corner but on the other two houses there is only one pillar on each after corner. Note that the masts, and also two derrick posts, are tapered. The robust crosstrees have three lightening holes in each of the arms.

The anchors are stowed in deep pockets with only the bottom of the anchor visible in the opening. The funnel is plated over just below the rim, as shown by the broken line on the detail sketch on the plan. Ventilators are of the mushroom type. The lifeboats were handled by gravity davits.

Colour Scheme

Hull: black above waterline to top of bulwark; side of poop and forecastle white, also their bulwarks, which have a black capping rail. Note that on the side of the forecastle the top of the black sweeps up in a flat curve from the level of the top of the Upper Deck bulwark at the break of the forecastle to a point just below the level of the forecastle deck at the stem. Inside bulwarks white. Boot topping pink.

Superstructure: white, inside bulwarks white.

Hatches: mid grey.

Masts, derrick posts, derricks: reddish brown; mast on wheelhouse white.

Decks: red oxide; superstructure decks wood planked; top of engine casing white.

Lifeboats: white, covers light grey.

Ventilators: white.

Davits: white.

Windlass: mid grey.

Glenogle

Photograph: J Byass

Glenogle (1962) Glen Line

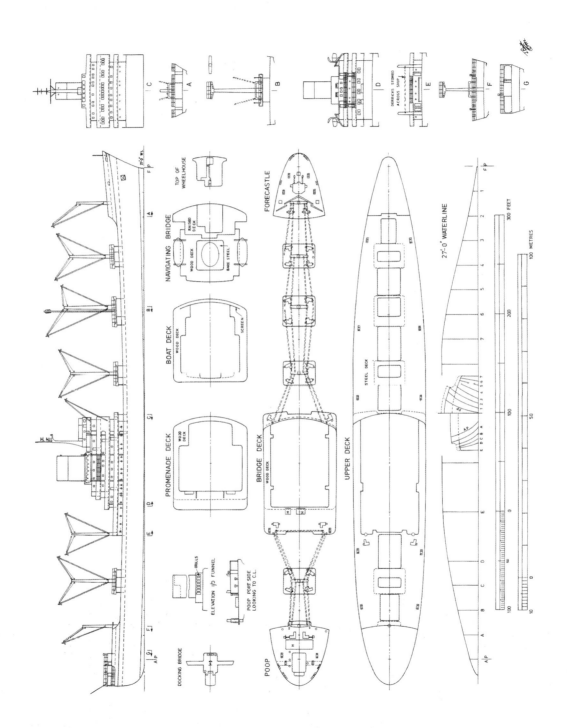

This photograph of *Glenogle* being launched gives a good idea of the hull shape forward and of the bow flare.

Photograph: author's collection

Winches: mid grey; the two at the after end of the Bridge Deck white.

Bollards, fairleads: black.

Funnel: red with black top.

Miscellaneous: lockers, etc, grey, accommodation ladder grey; breakwater white.

References

Illustrated articles, with small-scale GA plans are in the following technical journals: *The Motor Ship* (November 1962); *Shipbuilder & Marine Engine-Builder* (November 1962); *Shipbuilding & Shipping Record* (22 November 1962); *Shipping World* (22 November 1962).

The fleet history, and that of the Shire Line, is given in the book *Glen and Shire Lines* by Duncan Haws (Duncan Haws, 1991).

18

Haverford
(1901)

AMERICAN LINE

The *Haverford* was built in 1901 by John Brown & Co Ltd at Clydebank, Scotland, for the American Line's service between Liverpool and Philadelphia. Although officially owned by the International Navigation Company, itself part of the giant American-financed IMM, the ship was registered at Liverpool and flew the Red Ensign.

In appearance she was similar to many of the other vessels plying the North Atlantic at that time, yet in some ways she always seemed to have an air of elegance about her, the more so after the midship-house side plating above the Shelter Deck level was painted white. She remained on the service for which she was built until 1915 when she was requisitioned as a transport, only to be returned in 1916 to her regular route. In 1917 she was torpedoed off the Irish coast but made port, was repaired and put back into service. In 1921, while still on the same route, she was transferred to the White Star Line and continued on the same UK to USA run until the end of 1924, when she was sold to Italian shipbreakers.

The *Haverford's* sister ship *Merion*, for the same service, was completed at Clydebank in 1902. On the outbreak of war in 1914 she was purchased by the Admiralty and converted into the 'dummy battlecruiser' HMS *Tiger*. She was torpedoed and sunk in the Aegean in 1915.

Although her appearance belied the fact, the *Haverford* was able to carry nearly 2000 passengers and 10,000 tons of cargo – a very useful payload. In passing it is interesting to note that the early design plans of the ship show that she was intended to carry 150 cabin-class and 480 third-class passengers, general and refrigerated cargo and 744 head of cattle. Obviously there was a change of mind by the owners during building and the between-deck spaces were fitted out with accommodation, which enabled her to carry 1700 (sometimes more) third-class or steerage-class passengers; cabin or third class remained at 150 passengers. No cattle were carried.

The plan has been prepared from such shipbuilder's drawings as remain – rig, sectional profile, deck arrangements and midship section – and show the ship as built. The load draught was 30ft (9.0m), but the plan has been drawn to the 25ft (7.5m) waterline.

Modelling Notes

This is a straightforward model to build. Since there is but a single midship structure, the hull can be carved to the level of the Shelter Deck. Great care must be taken with the sheer line. There is not a great deal of flare on the hull at the fore end, and the counter stern appears slightly 'heavy' when seen in profile. The midship house is added as a separate unit; this has the added advantage of providing a clear, sharp line between hull and house when painting the hull if the model is to be shown with the side of this house painted white. The Boat Deck is carried out to the side of the ship and is supported by stanchions. The radial davits are fitted

Specification

Length overall:	547ft 8in (166.93m)
Length bp:	531ft 0in (161.84m)
Breadth:	59ft 3in (18.10m) (the hull had a tumblehome each side amidships of 12in)
Tonnage, gross:	11,635
Machinery:	twin screw with triple expansion engines developing 4200ihp
Speed:	13 knots

to the outside of the Boat Deck curtain plate, and terminate in heel castings fitted to the outside of the shell plating at the Promenade Deck level. There is an area of sparred decking outside the top of the house under the pair of boats forward and under the first pair aft of the midship house. Another narrow area of sparred decking supported by light pillars is fitted below the last two pairs of boats aft, the height above the Shelter Deck being the same as that of the midship house. An additional boat is stowed each side inboard of the aftermost boat on the Boat Deck.

The rake of each mast increases by equal amounts from the 7 degrees of the foremast to the 9 degrees of the jigger mast; the rake of the funnel is 8 degrees.

The cowl ventilators vary in size from 32in (0.8m) diameter abreast the foremast, 30in (0.75m) adjacent to the funnel, 28in (0.7m) under the first two pairs of boats abaft the midship house, 24in (0.6m) forward of the aftermost pair of boats to 18in (0.45m) for all the rest, except for those on skylights which are 12in (0.3m) diameter. These diameters refer to the stem or tube of the ventilator and not the cowl, which is at least one and a half times greater in diameter. The vertical twin-cylinder steam engine that drives the anchor windlass is fitted on the deck immediately abaft the windlass.

Colour Scheme

No colour specification was available for the vessel, but the following notes are based on the practices of the period. The funnel colours are, of course, correct for the American Line at that period.

Hull: black topsides, red below waterline. When built, the black was carried up to the level of the Promenade Deck. Later the side of the midship house above the Shelter Deck was painted white.

Deck erections: houses on Shelter Deck, ends of midship house have the upper half white and the lower half mid-brown (rust-brown); deckhouses elsewhere white, except wheelhouse which is mahogany.

Skylights: white, but engine room skylight black.

Bulwarks: white.

Hatches: black.

Bollards, fairleads: black.

Windlass, winches: black.

Boats, davits: white, boats have light grey covers.

Masts, derricks: mid brown (rust brown).

Ventilators: white, inside cowls red.

Funnel: black white band.

Decks: wood sheathed. Rectangular area on Boat Deck in way of funnel black.

References

Glasgow University Business Records Centre (see Appendix II, pp205–206) holds the few remaining shipbuilder's plans.

Haverford as completed, with the black topside paint carried up to the line of the Promenade Deck. Later, the hull above the level of the Shelter Deck was painted white.

Photograph: author's collection

Haverford (1901) American Line

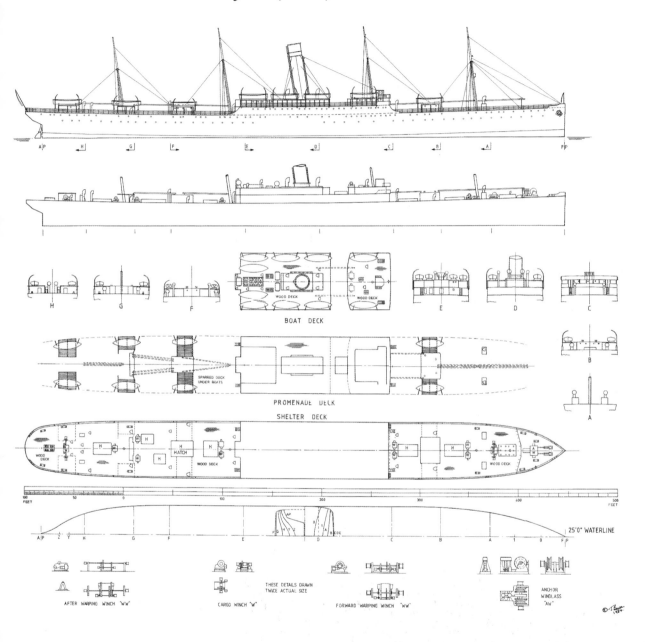

BOAT DECK

PROMENADE DECK

SHELTER DECK

25'0" WATERLINE

AFTER WARPING WINCH "WW"

CARGO WINCH "W"

THESE DETAILS DRAWN
TWICE ACTUAL SIZE

FORWARD WARPING WINCH "WW"

ANCHOR
WINDLASS
"AW"

19

Ivernia
(1900)

CUNARD STEAMSHIP COMPANY

Ivernia and her sister ship *Saxonia* were ordered by the Cunard Company at the end of the nineteenth century as part of a fleet-modernisation programme. The order for *Ivernia* went to C S Swan & Hunter at Newcastle and that for *Saxonia* to John Brown & Co, Clydebank. Both ships were intended for the Company's Liverpool to Boston service, and were designed with a big cargo-carrying capacity and fitted with accommodation for a large number of passengers in three classes. After making two voyages to New York as soon as she was completed, *Ivernia* settled down on her intended service, where she remained for the next ten years. Between 1910 and 1914 she made several voyages from Italy to New York, returning at times to the Liverpool–Boston run. On the outbreak of hostilities in 1914 the government requisitioned her for trooping duties and it was whilst on this service that she was torpedoed and sunk off Cape Matapan, Southern Greece on 1 January 1917. Her sister ship *Saxonia* survived the war, was refitted in 1920 and returned to the Company's service. She was sold for breaking up in 1925.

Ivernia and *Saxonia* were impressive-looking ships, with a long, sweeping sheer and four tall masts. But their outstanding feature was the immensely tall funnel, rising some 75ft (22.8m) above the Boat Deck and with a very prominent rim at the top.

Although referred to as sister ships, and generally similar in overall appearance, there were a number of noticeable external differences between the two ships. *Ivernia* did not have the cowl-topped derrick posts on the Shelter Deck forward in way of No 3 hatch, the small outrigger on the foremast or the flying bridge on top of the wheelhouse as fitted on *Saxonia*. On *Ivernia*, the boats forward of the bridge on the Bridge Deck, and again aft in way of the after deckhouse and in way of the jigger mast, were stowed on pedestals with their keels at top rail level. On *Saxonia* they

Specification	
Length overall:	600ft 0in (182.88m)
Length bp:	580ft 0in (176.78m)
Breadth mld:	64ft 6in (19.66m)
Draught:	29ft 0in (8.84m)
Tonnage, gross:	15,799 tons
Machinery:	two quadruple expansion engines, 12,000ihp; twin screw
Speed:	16 knots
Passengers:	160 first, 200 second, 1600 steerage

were on chocks on sparred decks level with the top of the deckhouses. The layout of the house tops on *Ivernia* was different to that of *Saxonia* and the latter had many more cowl ventilators at this location than *Ivernia*. On the Boat Deck on *Ivernia* the lifeboats were stowed with the keel in line with the edge of the deck, whereas on *Saxonia* they were stowed inboard. As a consequence of this the positions of the davits handling these boats was different on the two ships. The shape of the front of the bridge on *Ivernia* differed from that on *Saxonia*. *Ivernia* did not have a deckhouse at the base of the foremast, and the house at the fore end of the Bridge Deck was smaller. In plan view the shape of the after end of the Shelter Deck on *Ivernia* differed from that on *Saxonia*, being slightly more rounded. *Ivernia's* funnel was round whilst that on *Saxonia* was a flat-sided oval. *Ivernia's* masts were slightly taller than those on *Saxonia*.

Modelling Notes

The plan shows the ship as built. It will be easier to make the hull to the level of the Shelter Deck and add the long midship house as a separate piece. If this is made just fractionally narrower than the beam of the ship then the mounted shaving, which will be used to form the bulwark to the Bridge Deck, can be cut to the full depth of the house and glued along its side. It should be extended at each end to include the short lengths of bulwark beyond the ends of the house. In view of the number of deck stanchions between the Bridge Deck (i.e. the top of this house) and the Boat Deck, it may be easier to glue these in place along the inside of the bulwark before fitting the house on the Bridge Deck and before fitting the deck card that will form the Boat Deck. Note that this card is 1ft 0in (30cm) [to scale] wider each side than the Bridge Deck; also the tops of the deck stanchions are 1ft 0in inboard of the edge of the deck and the funnel sits on a raised casing about 1ft 0in high.

There is a large opening in the Shelter Deck forward to give light and air to the open promenade area on the deck below. This area occupies the full width of the ship, but as there are no openings in the ship's sides in way other than a number of portholes it will appear dark on the model when seen from above. It can be formed by cutting a hole in the hull of the model to a depth of a scale 8ft and in area at least ⅟₁₆in larger all round than the size of the opening in the deck. The edges of this hole should be painted matt black. The Shelter Deck forward is planked, so the whole area can be covered with a thin mounted shaving to represent the planking. The edge of this shaving should be kept a scale 15in inboard to form the waterway. As the waterway will be painted red oxide, it will be better if this area is given a coat of red oxide before this shaving is glued in place; this will ensure a good clean, sharp edge. The opening in the deck shaving in way of the above-mentioned opening must be cut out before the shaving is fitted, and cut to the size shown on the plan, and not to the enlarged size of the hole. There is another similar, but smaller, opening in the Shelter Deck aft and this, and the deck, should be treated in the same way.

Two deckhouses on the Shelter Deck aft and the large house on the Boat Deck have a projecting moulding running round the top of the house. This can be represented by covering the top of a house with a piece of thin card cut to project fractionally beyond the edge of the block representing the house. This is indicated on the drawing by a broken line round the house in plan view.

The Cunard liner *Ivernia* as completed. The small white rectangle on the side of the ship below the forward boat is an open door.
Photograph: author's collection

Ivernia (1900) Cunard Steamship Company

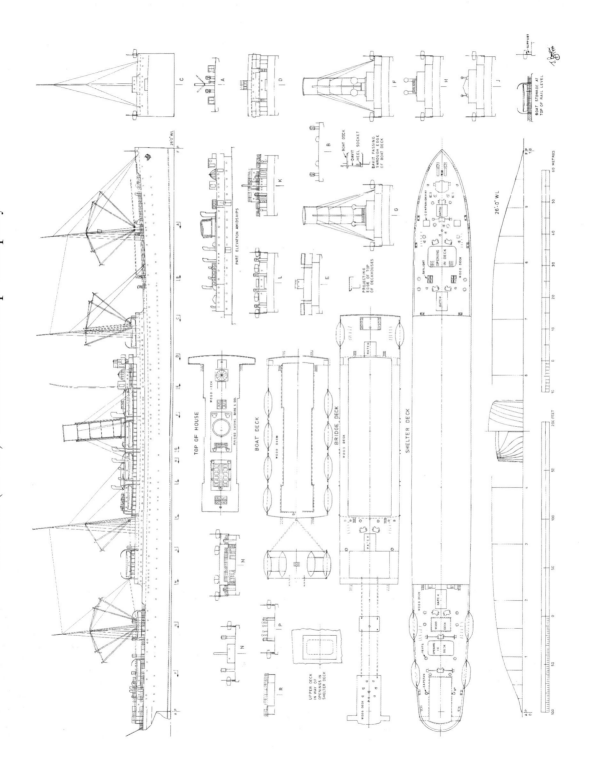

The derricks for the foremast stow parallel both to the ship's centre line and to the deck. Their stowed position has been omitted on the plan view of the Shelter Deck for clarity. Those for the mainmast stow vertically against the mast. Just aft of the wheelhouse is a cupola (clear glass dome) providing light to the space below; this should be made of a piece of polished clear Perspex.

The lifeboats are stowed on half chocks and on the Boat Deck with the keel in line with the edge of the deck, while on the Bridge Deck on the top of the house at the after end. Elsewhere they are stowed on pedestals with the keel just above and over the top of a bulwark or the guardrails. The davits for these latter boats are fitted in pedestals just inside the bulwark or guardrails. The davits for the boats on the Boat Deck pass through the deck just inside its edge, with the heel in a heel socket fitted outside the Bridge Deck bulwark at the level of the Bridge Deck. The davits for the boat each side of the house on the after end of the Bridge Deck pass through a fitting outside the forward and after ends of the deck on the top of the house, and have the heel in a heel socket outside the bulwark on the Bridge Deck at the level of that deck.

Colour Scheme

Hull: black to level of Shelter Deck, and including the bow bulwark; red below the waterline (Humbrol 174); narrow white ribband dividing red and black.
Superstructure: white, deckhouses white, wheelhouse mahogany. When the two ships first entered service, the side of the midship superstructure from the line of the Shelter Deck up to a height of 3ft 6in (1.07m – the height of the short bulwarks at either end) was painted golden brown (Humbrol 62).
Masts, derricks: golden brown.
Ventilators: white, inside cowls red.
Lifeboats, davits: white; boats have narrow mahogany sheerstrake, plain canvas covers without tabs.
Windlass, winches: black.
Bollards, fairleads: black.
Hatches: golden brown, black tops.
Funnel: Cunard red (Humbrol 174 is the nearest), black top, three narrow black bands.
Decks: wood planked; shallow casing under funnel black.
Miscellaneous: skylights on house tops black, elsewhere skylights white, water tanks white.

References

The Marine Engineer (1 May 1900) contains an illustrated article on *Ivernia*; an article in *Engineering* (12 September 1899) includes a small-scale GA plan (sectional profile with 'chopped off' funnels and masts) and deck arrangements; a further article appears in a later issue of *Engineering* (21 September 1900); *The Engineer* (6 April 1900) contains a useful article; The Glasgow University Business Records Centre (see Appendix II, pp205–206) has some of the shipbuilder's plans of *Saxonia* (Yard No 339).

20

Kosmos III
(1947)

WHALE-OIL FACTORY SHIP

For 14 years following her completion in 1947 *Kosmos III* was one of the largest active whale-oil factory ships under the Norwegian flag. She was built by Gotaverken at Gothenburg for Anders Jahre of Sandefjord, Norway, being finished just in time to leave, within a few days of being handed over, for the start of the 1947–8 Atlantic whaling season. At that time the season was limited to four months (December to March) hence the rush. The factory ship processes the whales caught by the attendant fleet of catchers, stows the products on board and transports them home at the end of the season.

The plan is of the vessel as completed. Some years later a shelter was built over the two large winches on the Winch Bridge, the Boat Deck was extended to the stern and the existing deckhouse on it similarly extended. Two new deckhouses were also built on it. These additions gave her a somewhat heavy appearance aft, spoiling what had been quite a reasonably balanced profile.

Kosmos III was sold to Tayo Gyogyo KK of Tokyo in August 1961 and renamed *Nisshin Maru 3*. She was still around in 1993, but under the ownership of Nippon Kyodo Hogel KK also of Tokyo. The Anders Jahers company is no longer in existence.

Modelling Notes

The hull is without shear. Another point of interest is that there is no tumblehome. In fact the reverse is the case. The sides of the hull slope inwards from 78ft (23.77m) beam at upper deck level to 74ft (23.2m) at the bottom. Were the ship to be caught in ice any pressure would tend to squeeze the hull upwards, whereas under similar circumstances one with a tumblehome could well be locked in. The breadth at the waterline would be about 76ft (23.8m).

The main part of the hull will be a rectangular block to which must be added a block for the poop, one for the lower

Specification	
Length overall:	638ft 6in (194.61m)
Length bp:	598ft 0in (182. 27m)
Breadth at deck:	78ft 0in (23.77m)
Draught:	34ft 0in (10.36m)
Tonnage, deadweight:	23,500 tons
Machinery:	Diesel, 8300 ihp, single screw
Speed:	14 knots
Complement:	400

forecastle and a shorter one on that for the upper forecastle. The inboard end of each piece must be finished and painted before being glued in place. However, before the one for the poop is fitted the skidway, i.e. the passage along which the whales are hauled to the upper or flensing deck (note: the area of the upper deck between the winch bridge and the poop is generally referred to as the flensing deck), must be cut in the hull block. As can be seen on the plan this runs down from the deck in a gentle curve to the level of the 34ft (10.3m) waterline. The Poop Deck must have a section 18ft (5.55m) wide cut out of its centre from the fore end to the winches forward point some 8ft (2.5m) forward of the AP. The underside of this solid end must have a curve cut in it to match that of the skidway. On the profile these two curves are shown as broken lines. On the Cabin Deck aft, i.e. the deck below the Upper Deck, there is an opening each side in the hull, with a bulwark and three vertical stanchions. Once all three blocks are in place the hull can be carved to shape. In profile the stem has a very gentle curve, but the transom is straight until just above the waterline

This photograph of *Kosmos III* at sea was taken several years after she was built and shows that a number of changes have been made.

The house on top of the deckhouses on the Boat Deck, and the shelter on the winch deck amidships are later additions.

Photographs courtesy of SkyFotos

Kosmos III (1947) Whale Oil Factory Ship

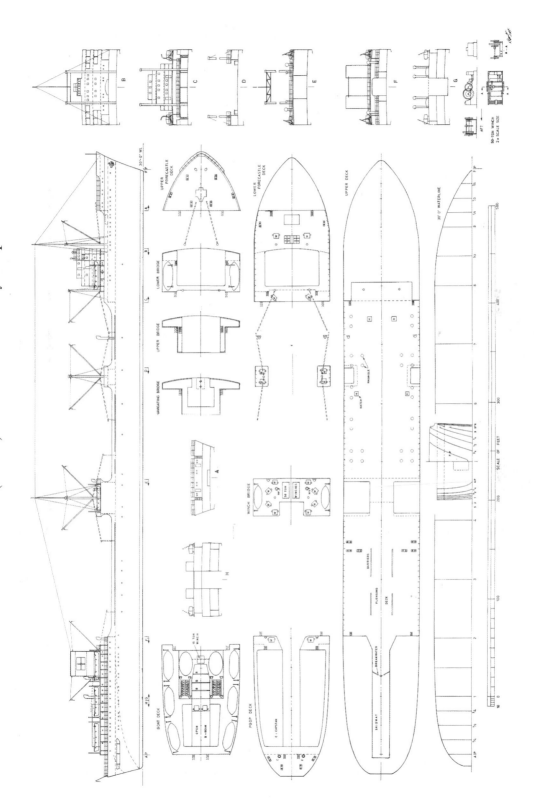

where it begins to curve under. The edges of the skidway opening in the stern are slightly rounded.

The bridge structure forward, the poop and the various deck erections are straightforward. At Boat Deck level the open top of the skidway has a short platform across it at mid length on which are two winches. Forward of this platform the opening is crossed by three rectangular beams. The Poop Deck is wood sheathed (planked) except for an area at the fore end in way of the funnels and engine skylights. All other decks are wood sheathed, including the upper deck. The top of the winch bridge and the top of the two small houses forward of it are bare steel, as is the skidway. The latter has a removable breakwater about 3ft (0.9m) high towards its forward end.

The Upper Deck bulwarks have a long continuous gap between the bottom of the bulwark plating and the top of the sheerstrake (i.e. deck edge) for much of their length. They are fitted with the usual plate brackets or stays, spaced about 5½ft (1.65m) apart.

The 28 small circles on the Upper Deck are manhole covers, which can be represented by paper discs glued in place. The six rectangles are access hatches, with coamings 3ft (0.9m) high. On the flensing deck forward of the skidway are four short lengths of protective barriers, two port and two starboard, about 3ft high and 18in (0.45m) thick; their ends are not vertical but snapped off at about 60 degrees.

The derricks stow as shown on the drawing. The foremast and the mainmast are each carried on a latticework gantry fitted at the top of the associated derrick posts immediately below their mushroom tops. The lifeboat on each side of the lower bridge is carried under crescent-type davits. All of the remaining boats are handled by davits that have straight upper arms rather than curved ones. The funnels are painted over about 18in (0.45m) below the top, with three exhaust outlets in each. A light beam runs between the two funnels, as shown on one of the sections on the plan. The funnel insignia is the company's houseflag, and this is found on both sides of each funnel.

Colour Scheme

Hull: light to medium grey from waterline to the top of the poop deck and top of the lower forecastle deck, above which it is white; boot topping green.
Superstructure: white.
Deckhouses: white; tops of winch bridge and two adjacent small houses black.
Bulwarks: white, as are the four small protective barriers on the flensing deck.
Windlass, winches: black.
Bollards: black.
Lifeboats, davits: white, boat covers light buff.
Ventilators: white, blue inside cowls.
Masts, derrick posts, derricks: white.
Decks: planked, except for area on boat deck in way of funnels and skylights and tops of winch bridge and two small adjacent to house which are black.
Funnels: black with broad red band in the centre of which on both sides of each funnel is the company's houseflag. The flag is a rectangle of white with a white five-pointed star within a blue disk at the center of a vertical blue cross.
Miscellaneous: skylights white; access hatches on upper deck coamings black, tops white; skidway black, sides and overhead white.

References

Articles with small-scale general arrangement (GA) plans and photographs can be found in: *Shipbuilder & Marine Engine-Builder* (January 1948); *Shipbuilding & Shipping Record* (20 November 1947); *Motor ship* (November 1947) which has an article only; *The Motor Ship* (January 1949) which contains an article with a small-scale GA plan of the similar but larger vessel *Kosmos V*.

Skyfotos (see Appendix II, pp205–206) have several photographs of the ship taken after the above alterations had been made.

21

Leicestershire (1909)

BIBBY BROS

The *Leicestershire* was a good example of the elegant pro-file of four tall masts and single slender funnel, which was first adopted by the Bibby Line some years earlier. The vessel was built in 1909 by Harland & Wolff at Belfast (Yard No 403) for the owner's service between Liverpool and Ceylon and Burma.

Upon completion *Leicestershire* ran steadily on that route until 1914 when, following the outbreak of war, she was taken up as a troop transport for four months before being returned to her owner's service. In 1917 she was again req-uisitioned and was not handed back until the war was over. Following a major overhaul in 1919 she went on to their Rangoon service, where she remained until 1930. In that year she was purchased by the British National Exhibition Ship Co Ltd to operate as a floating exhibition for British goods. Renamed *British Exhibition* after conversion, she never sailed in her new role as the company went into liqui-dation in 1932. After being laid up for a year she was sold to Egyptian interests, renamed *Zamzam*, and used in the pil-grim trade between Cairo and Jeddah. In 1934 she changed hands again, going to another Cairo company who contin-ued to run her intermittently in the pilgrim trade. In 1941, when on a voyage from New York to Alexandria, she was intercepted by the German raider *Tamesis* (one of the names used by the German raider only ever identified as 'Raider C') in the South Atlantic. Despite the fact that she was a neutral ship, and displaying neutral colours, she was shelled and sunk. A full account of this affair appeared in the American magazine *Life* (23 June 1941) and also in Volume 11 (June 1951) of *Sea Breezes* under the title 'The *Zamzam* Incident'.

The plan has been based on shipbuilder's drawings and shows the ship as built. During the 1919 overhaul, among much other work, the masts were shortened slightly and light topgallant masts were fitted (making her appear even

Specification

Length overall:	481ft 6in (146.8m)
Length bp:	467ft 3in (142.4m)
Breadth mld:	54ft 4in (16.5m)
Draught:	27ft 8in (8.4m)
Tonnage, gross:	8059 tons
Machinery:	twin screw quadruple expansion
Speed:	15 knots

loftier). She was still carrying these at the time of her loss. A large deckhouse was fitted forward of the mizzen mast, and two derrick posts were fitted just forward of the funnel to serve a new hatchway.

Modelling Notes

A study of the plan will show that the sheer can be cut to at the level of the Promenade (forecastle) Deck, with the two wells being formed by a cut down to the line of the Upper Deck. The bulwarks for these should be cut from paper-mounted shavings and glued to the deck edge. At the after end of the long midship house on the Upper Deck (part of the hull block) is an opening on the starboard side only. There is no bulwark at the bow. The stem bar extends about 15in (0.5mm) above deck level, with the top rounded off. On the edge of the deck each side immediately abaft this extended stem bar is a short fairlead.

The deckhouses should be cut from stripwood reduced in thickness to the correct deck height (with due allowance being made for the card to be used to form any overhanging deck). The houses on the Promenade Deck have narrow light-and-air casings at intervals along the sides. Note that the houses on the Boat Deck are of three different heights. The after part of the aftermost house on the Boat Deck is arranged as a verandah lounge, open at its after end. Across this open end is a low bulwark 3ft 6in (1.06m) high, with two access openings and light tubular stanchions set at intervals between the top of this bulwark and the deckhead. Across the fore end of the Boat Deck is a bulwark, the centre part of which is increased in height to form a screen with windows. When preparing this for the model the centre section is extended to form the similar screen across the front of the Navigation Bridge above.

The boats are stowed under radial davits. Those serving the forward and aftermost boats each side are mounted in pedestals on the deck. The forward boat is carried above rail height, turned outboard and secured by gripes. The remaining boat davits are fitted outside the Boat Deck curtain plate, with the heel of each resting in a socket attached to the shell plating at Promenade Deck level. The one slightly

tedious task is the fitting of the closely spaced deck stanchions along each side of the Promenade Deck.

Colour Scheme

Hull: black to Promenade Deck level, red below waterline; narrow yellow ribband along each side at the level of the top of the Upper Deck bulwarks.

Superstructure: white; the lower half of the house ends on the Upper Deck, and the sides and ends of the houses on the Promenade Deck and Poop mid brown.

Ventilators: on engine/boiler casing black, on forecastle mid-buff, elsewhere white; inside of all cowls white.

Masts, derricks, derrick post vents, anchor crane: mid buff (Humbrol colour 'sand').

Funnel: 'Bibby' pink with black top ('Bibby' pink is BS 2-032 in British Standard Colour Chart BS 1660 of 1950; the nearest Humbrol colour would be 'Flesh' but this is slightly lighter).

Boats and davits: white, covers (which do not have triangular side tabs) very light grey.

Leicestershire as completed in 1909.

Photograph: Bibby Bros

Leicestershire (1909) Bibby Bros

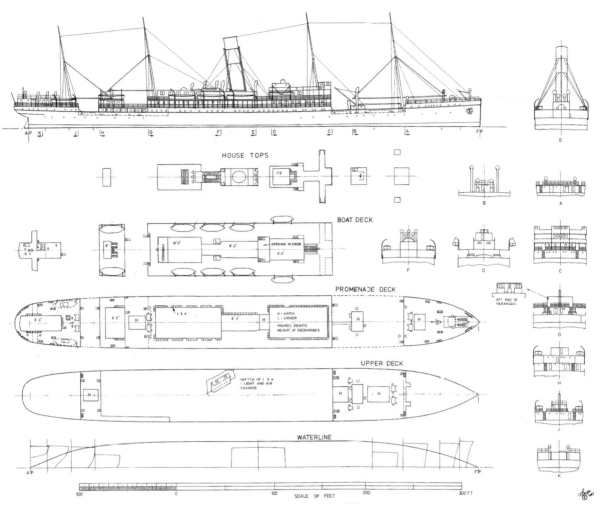

Engine room skylight: black.

Hatches: sides mast colour, tops black.

Inside bulwarks: on Upper Deck mid-brown, elsewhere white.

Decks: teak planked; top of the engine/boiler casing black; after half of the top of the house on the poop bare steel, i.e. black, the other (forward) half teak planked.

References

As for Bibby Bros' *Derbyshire* (see p110).

22

Mauretania
(1939)

CUNARD LINE

Mauretania (Yard No 1029) was built by Cammell, Laird & Co Ltd at Birkenhead for what the owners, Cunard White Star Ltd, referred to as their secondary line service between Southampton and New York. The vessels on this service were luxuriously fitted out; the only difference between them and the large express liners on the route, apart from size, was that their service speed was lower. Although she was, and is, frequently referred to as *Mauretania II* to differentiate her from her famous predecessor of that name, this suffix is not part of her official name.

She was a distinctive vessel, with good lines, raked stem, uncluttered superstructure with a curved front and two well-raked funnels and masts. Her general appearance was often regarded as being the prototype for the *Queen Elizabeth*, then in the early stages of construction on the Clyde.

Mauretania made her maiden voyage in May 1939 and shortly after the outbreak of World War II was requisitioned for service as a troopship, and in that capacity carried service personnel all over the world for six years. When she was released late in 1946 her owners immediately sent her back to the builders for a complete overhaul and refit. Upon its completion she resumed her normal North Atlantic service in 1947, but before long began winter cruising out of New York. Then in the 1950s and early 1960s she combined more and more cruising with her regular voyages on the Atlantic service. During her annual overhaul in 1962 she was painted in the three shades of green first adopted by Cunard for their cruising liner *Caronia* in 1949, thus bringing her in line with that cruising partner.

Early in 1965 she was withdrawn from service and sold to Messrs Thomas W Ward for breaking up, finally berthing at Inverkeithing, Scotland, on 23 November 1965.

Although she lacked the aura that surrounded her prede-

Specification	
Length overall:	771ft 10in (235.0m)
Length bp:	732ft 0in (223.1m)
Breadth mld:	89ft 1in (27.1m)
Draught:	30ft 10in (9.4m)
Tonnage, gross:	35,739 tons
Machinery:	single-reduction geared turbines, 40,000shp, twin screw
Speed:	22 knots
Passengers:	486 cabin class, 390 tourist, 502 third

cessor she was, nevertheless, a distinctive vessel with a reputation for steadiness and always a favourite with passengers. But she became a casualty of the times, due mainly to the changing pattern of travel.

Modelling Notes

There is more than one way in which the basic hull can be made. The sheer can be carved to the level of the Sun Deck throughout the length of the hull block, and then cut down at the ends to the different deck levels. But whilst this does give a flush surface to the sides of most of the central part of the superstructure, it does involve quite a bit of work at the ends. Alternatively, the sheer of the hull block can be cut throughout its length to Main Deck level and then, at the after end, cut down to the level of A Deck from the point X–X right to the stern. After marking the outline of the Main Deck and A Deck on the top of the block, and of the waterline on the underside, the hull can be carved to shape,

Mauretania as completed.

This shows *Mauretania* sometime after her post-war overhaul and refit. Note the radar equipment on top of the wheelhouse.

checking constantly with templates cut to the section shapes shown on the body plan. The pocket, or recess, on each side of the bow in which the anchors are stowed should be cut.

Prepare a piece of wood equal to the thickness of the deckhouse on A deck less the thickness of the deck card which will cover the after end of this deck from point X–X aft. Paint the edges white and glue in place. In view of its shape it may be easier to make it in two pieces, the broad section and the narrow tail, rather than cut it as a single piece.

The long house on the Main Deck can be formed by a single piece of wood, with the ends shaped as on the plan, but the thickness must be reduced by that of the deck card which will cover it. Again it may be easier to add as separate pieces the narrower extension at the after end and also the small one at the fore end; the deck card will cover the butt joint. The rest of the main superstructure can be built up in the same way up to, and including, the house at the fore end of the Sports Deck and the wheelhouse above. Although this is the easiest way to build the superstructure, it is essential that great care be taken over the thickness of each of the various component parts to ensure that the overall height from the Main Deck to the top of the Sports Deck, and again to the top of the wheelhouse, is not exceeded. At the after end of the Sun Deck there is an area of raised deck 2ft (0.6m) high and a similar raised area, also 2ft high, at the after end of the Promenade Deck.

The side of the superstructure should be covered with a piece of mounted wood shaving from Main Deck level to Sun Deck level. The fore end must be cut to the shape shown on the plan and the after end cut to include the bulwark each side of A Deck and the Main Deck. As the various decks at the fore end of the superstructure are stepped, the front of each deck can be faced with paper, which is extended above deck level to form the bulwark. At the fore end of the Sun Deck there is a full-height screen each side, extending half way across the space between the ship's side and the side of the deckhouse. It is advisable to fit this before adding the piece of very thin card, shaped like an inverted 'T', which forms the short length of bulwark on the Sun Deck at that point and also the support to the wing of the Navigating Bridge. This completes the work on the hull and the main part of the superstructure. If desired the hull can be painted before proceeding with the rest of the work.

A number of points should be made about the fittings. The funnels are plated over a few feet below the top, the plating being pierced by a number of outlets as shown. These can be made by carving a piece of wood to the cross section of the funnels, cutting off pieces to the level of the internal plating and wrapping a strip of paper round each one, keeping the top edge above the top of the wood to form the rim of the funnel. The top of each of the three cargo hatches is curved in cross section transversely. Some of the mushroom-top ventilators have circular tops while others have square tops.

The inboard ends of the trackways of the gravity davits rest on top of the house on the Sun Deck, except for the last three trackways each side, the ends of which are supported by A-shaped frames. A gangway, in three sections, runs along the top of the inboard ends of the davit trackways. This gangway extends beyond the after end of the deckhouse and along the tops of those davit trackways supported by the A-shaped frames. The boat winches are sited on this gangway, which is increased in width in way of these winches. Columbus-type davits are fitted to handle the boats at the after end of the Promenade Deck.

At the fore end of the Main Deck there are trays between the hawse pipes and the cable lifters on which the anchor cable lies. These can be made from strips of paper and painted black before being glued in position.

Colour Scheme

Hull: black to the level of the top of A deck bulwark; boot topping red, with a narrow white ribband dividing red from black topside paint; white above A-Deck bulwark.

Superstructure: white; deckhouses white; top of funnel casings and of foremast house light grey; louvres in the sides of the engine casings light grey (Humbrol 64).

Masts, derrick posts, derricks: golden brown (Humbrol 62)

Ventilators: white.

Lifeboats, davits: white, boat covers light grey (Humbrol 64); boat winches white.

Cable lifters, capstans: light grey (Humbrol 64).

Winches: light grey (Humbrol 64).

Bollards, fairleads: black.

Hatches: light grey (Humbrol 64).

Funnels: Cunard red (Humbrol 174), black top, two narrow black bands.

Decks: all wood sheathed (planked).

Miscellaneous: anchor crane white, cable trays black.

References

Shipbuilder & Marine Engine-Builder (June 1939) contains a technical article with small-scale general arrangement plan. This was reprinted as a hardback, with additional new material by Mark Warren (Patrick Stephens Ltd, 1989 [ISBN 1-85260-233-3]).

Mauretania (1939) Cunard Line

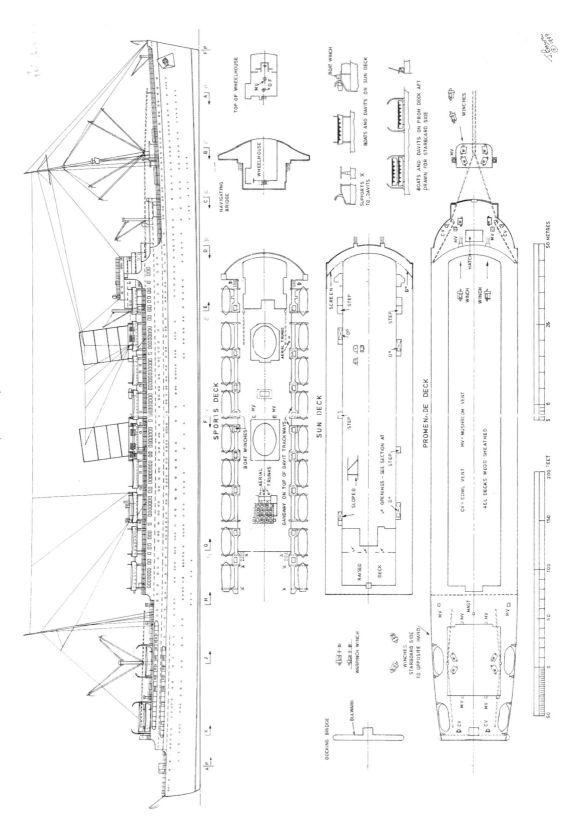

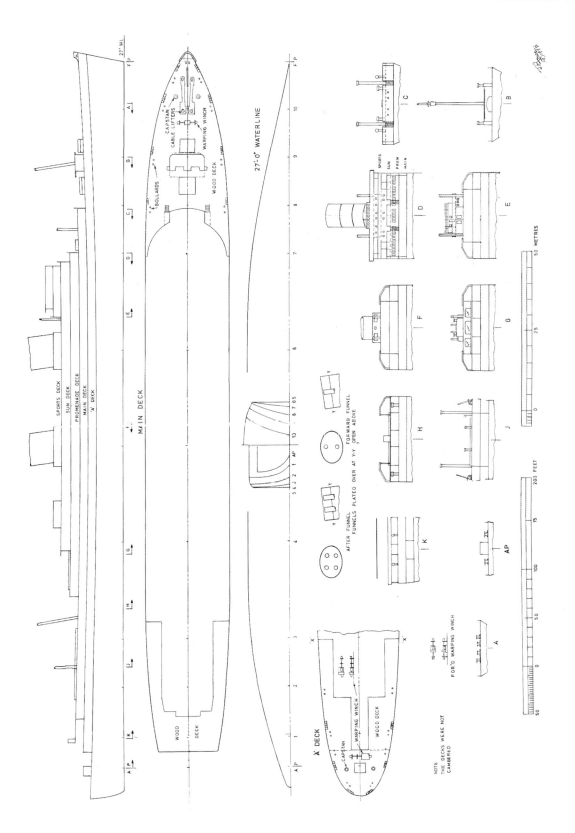

23

Miltiades (1902)

ABERDEEN LINE

The clipper-stemmed steamship *Miltiades* and her sister ship *Marathon* were two fine-looking ships. Indeed it was often said that their already favourable appearance was enhanced when they were lengthened and given a second funnel. The ships were built in 1903 by Alexander Stephen & Sons at Linthouse in Glasgow (Yard Nos 401 and 402 respectively) for the Aberdeen Line's (George Thompson & Co) service between London and Sydney. In 1912, to take advantage of the considerable increase in the Australian emigrant traffic, first *Marathon* and then *Miltiades* were sent back to their builders to be lengthened. They were cut through just forward of the boiler room and a new 51ft 9in (15.77m) section was inserted. To balance the appearance of the ship a second (dummy) funnel was fitted.

Both ships spent some time during World War I on trooping duties, and both survived. They returned to the Australian run after the war but in 1921 were transferred to the Royal Mail Steam Packet Company, when they were renamed *Orcana* and *Oruba* respectively. The RMSP Company allocated then to the Pacific Steam Navigation Company's West Coast of South America service. They proved to be too expensive to run, so were withdrawn in 1923 and laid up. The following year *Miltiades* was sold to Dutch shipbreakers and *Marathon* to German shipbreakers.

Modelling Notes

The hull should be carved to the top of the poop, bridge and forecastle, and cut away down to the Upper Deck forward and aft to form the wells. The forward part of the midship house must be cut away on each side for a short distance to form an open promenade, as shown on the plan. When shaping the hull particular care must be taken to obtain the correct curve to the clipper stem and to form the step down from the forecastle deck at its fore end to accommodate the short spike bowsprit. The figurehead (of a hel-

Specification

Length overall:	490ft 0in (149.35m)
Length bp:	454ft 9in (138.65m)
Breadth mld:	55ft 1in (16.79m)
Draught:	27ft 0in (8.23m)
Tonnage, gross:	6795 tons
Machinery:	Triple expansion, twin screw
Speed:	15 knots

meted Greek warrior on *Miltiades*) can be built up with a few spots of a suitable medium. There is a short length of low bulkhead plating about 18in (0.45m) high around the curved fore end of the forecastle deck. The two trail boards each side of the stem can be cut from black-painted paper, with the decorative scrollwork added in gold paint. Bulwarks made from paper-mounded wood shaving enclose both wells.

There are only five small deckhouses forming the superstructure, plus another on the poop. These are rectangular, but two have one end slightly curved. The Boat Deck has a curtain plate about 15in (0.38m) deep, so the material used for the deckhouses on the Bridge Deck will have to be reduced in thickness by this amount to compensate for the card used to form the overhanging deck.

On the Boat Deck the funnel is on a rectangular casing 18in (0.38m) in height, which has a narrow light-and-air skylight along each side. Aft of the funnel there is another raised casing of the same height with a narrow light-and-air skylight across its after end. Across the fore end is a fiddley (stokehold) grating. Apart from the engine room skylight at the after end of the Boat Deck, there are three other skylights on this deck, plus another two on the poop.

There are 12 steam winches and 14 derricks. The cargo hatches are covered with tarpaulins. Quadrant-type davits handle the lifeboats. All decks are planked, with a 12in (0.3m) waterway (21in [0.53m] in the well decks forward and aft). On the plan many of the cowl ventilators have been omitted from the outboard profile for clarity; their heights are shown on the sectional profile. Looking along the line of stanchions between the Bridge Deck and the Boat Deck it will be seen that in two places a full-height stanchion is missing; this is correct (not a draughting error).

Colour Scheme

Hull: dark green (Hooker's Green) to the level of the top of the well deck bulwarks, pale cream above that point to deck level, boot topping salmon pink; ends of poop, bridge and forecastle – lower half mid-brown, upper half pale cream; inside of well deck bulwarks mid-brown; figurehead white, trail boards black with gold scrollwork.

Superstructure: sides and ends of houses on Bridge Deck and Poop, lower half mid-brown, upper half pale cream; house on Boat Deck pale cream; wheelhouse, Navigating Bridge bulwark and wing cabs, bulwark across fore end of Boat Deck, teak; boiler casing under funnel black.

Hatches: coamings mid-brown.
Masts, derrick posts, derricks, spike bowsprit: buff.
Lifeboats and davits: white.
Ventilators: white, four large cowl ventilators by funnel buff, inside of all cowls red.
Windlass: black.
Winches: black.
Bollards, fairleads: black.
Funnel: buff.
Miscellaneous: engine room skylights black, other skylights teak; light-and-air skylights on side/end of low casings on Boat Deck same colour as casings; anchor crane white.

References

The National Maritime Museum in Greenwich holds a number of builder's plans. The lines plan and the GA plan of the decks are for the ships as built, but the rigging plan supplied for *Miltiades* was for the ship after lengthening. As this shows clearly where the new section was inserted (its frames are marked with letters, not numerals), it presents no problems when used in conjunction with the deck plans. The Historic Photographs Section of the museum has two excellent photographs of *Miltiades* lying off Gravesend, one almost full broadside and the other about three-quarter port view, and

The fine graceful lines of *Miltiades* are well shown here.

Photograph: author's collection

Miltiades (1902) Aberdeen Line

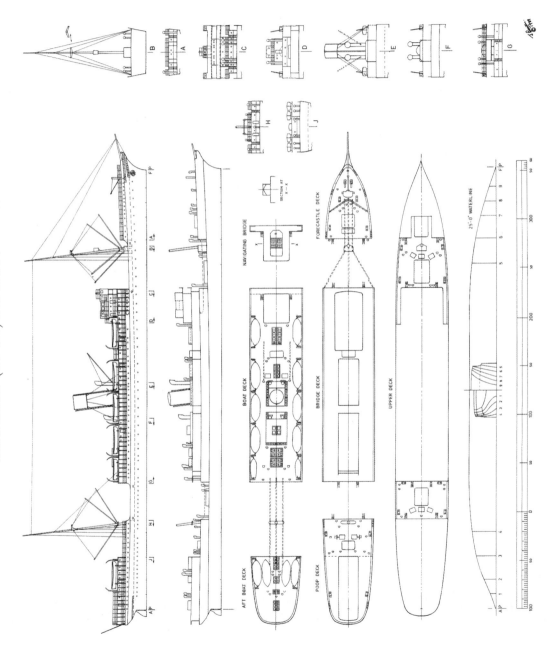

Marathon after lengthening and the addition of the second funnel.

Photograph: author's collection

an almost full port broadside view of *Marathon*. These are in the Gould Collection and are particularly sharp and clear.

Sea Breezes Volume 8 (November 1949) and *North Star to Southern Cross* by John M Maber (Prescot, Lancs: T Stephenson & Sons Ltd, 1967) contain some notes about the ships; the *Shipbuilder & Shipping Record* (28 May 1935, p707) features an article on *Marathon* in the series 'Ships That Made History' (note: this article covers the life of the ship and is not a technical article); the Science Museum in London has a builder's model of *Miltiades*.

24

Normannia
(1890)

HAMBURG AMERIKA LINE

Towards the end of the 1880s the Hamburg Amerika Line (Hapag) was falling behind their rival, Norddeutscher Lloyd (NDL), on the North Atlantic express service between Germany and New York. To remedy this state of affairs the company decided to build four liners with a service speed in excess of that of their competitors. Initially they ordered two ships, the *Augusta Victoria* (this unfortunate erroneous spelling of the name was quietly corrected to *Auguste Victoria* some years later) from the Vulcan yard at Stettin, and the *Columbia* from Laird Bros at Birkenhead. These were followed soon afterwards by orders for a second pair. The company went again to Vulcan for the *Furst Bismarck*, but placed the order for *Normannia* with the Fairfield Shipbuilding & Engineering Co in Glasgow (Yard No 343). The first two ships were completed in 1889 and the final two in 1890.

Although generally similar in design the four were not sister ships. All had three funnels, but whereas the first pair had three masts, the second pair had only two. In addition, *Furst Bismarck* and *Normannia* were some 40ft (12.0m) longer and 2ft (0.6m) wider in breadth. As might be expected with three shipbuilders being involved there were other minor differences. The funnels of the Laird and Fairfield vessels were slightly taller, and some of the boats were stowed with their keels at rail height while some were stowed on skid decks at deckhouse height.

All four ships settled down on the owner's Hamburg to New York express service with an average speed of 19 knots, which bettered that (by 1 knot) of the NDL steamers on the same service.

In 1898, following the outbreak of the Spanish–American war, *Normannia* and *Columbia* were sold to the Spanish Government for conversion to armed merchant cruisers. *Normannia* was renamed *Patriota*, but the work of fitting her for her new role was so slow that the war was over before

Specification	
Length overall:	518ft 0in (157.88m)
Length bp:	500ft 0in (152.4m)
Breadth:	57ft 6in (17.52m)
Draught:	24ft 0in (7.32m)
Tonnage, gross:	8246 tons
Machinery:	Two triple expansion engines, 16,000ihp, twin screw
Speed:	19 knots
Passengers, as built:	420 first class, 172 second, 722 third

it was completed, and she was put to one side. In 1899 she was seized by the French Government to recover an outstanding debt for coal supplied to Spain and was handed over to the Compagnie Generale Transatlantique (CGT or French Line) as a replacement for their recently lost *La Bourgogne*. They rebuilt the accommodation, with little noticeable alteration to her general external appearance, and renamed her *L'Aquitane*. She was placed on the company's Havre to New York service, where she remained until withdrawn in 1905 and sold to shipbreakers at Bo'ness, Scotland.

Modelling Notes

As the drawing shows, the hull has only a very short length of parallel body amidships, and there is little concavity to the flare of the bow sections. Both forecastle and poop have a slight turtleback.

The hull should be carved to the line of the Upper Deck,

Normannia as completed.   *Photograph: author's collection*

with the poop and forecastle added as separate pieces before the rest of the hull is carved. As the Forecastle Deck extends some way aft of the houses below it, the underside of the block for the forecastle can be cut away for a short distance to form the open end. A very thin piece must be left to represent the overhanging part of the deck, and an allowance must be made for forming the turtleback. This area must be painted before the piece is glued in place. Once this has been done, the sides of the hull can be carved to shape.

The long house on the Upper Deck can be made in one piece, but will have to be well fastened down to ensure good contact with the Upper Deck throughout its length. Note that the sides of the house are not straight but parallel to the sides of the hull. When cutting the card to form the Promenade Deck, it should be extended at the fore end to include the piece that runs forward over the deckhouse on the Upper Deck to meet up with the forecastle. The two narrow gangways at the after end leading to the Poop Deck can also be incorporated.

Because of their different widths it is better to make each of the houses on the Promenade Deck as separate units. When in place they can be covered with two pieces of thin card to hide the butts. Two pieces are needed because of the gap between the houses abreast the second boat. The sides and exposed ends of all houses must be painted, and doors,

portholes added, before the houses are fitted on the model.

The lifeboats are stowed on skid decks, which are level with the tops of the adjacent deckhouses and supported by three stanchions each. These can be made of wire, which should be bent over at the top to form the beams on which the sparred deck (which can be represented by a piece of card) was laid. The inboard ends of these beams should be secured to the top of the deckhouse. In way of the second boat, the inboard end of the forward stanchion is extended and fastened to a short beam running fore and aft between the ends of the two deckhouses. Each boat was stowed on its chocks on a support, which had light timber sparring fixed fore and aft atop it. On the drawing two boats on the starboard side have been left off to show this sparring and how it was extended between those two skid decks to form a narrow connecting walkway. The sparring under the other boats was generally similar. Ordinary radial davits set in pedestals on the Promenade Deck were fitted to handle the boats. A small boat was stowed on deck at the starboard after end of the Promenade Deck. A collapsible boat was stowed each side on the Bridge Deck immediately inboard of the fifth boat.

Just forward of the forward funnel a flying bridge, some 12ft (3.7m) above the Bridge Deck, was supported by pillars and stanchions and housed a binnacle and four

Normannia (1890) Hamburg Amerika Line

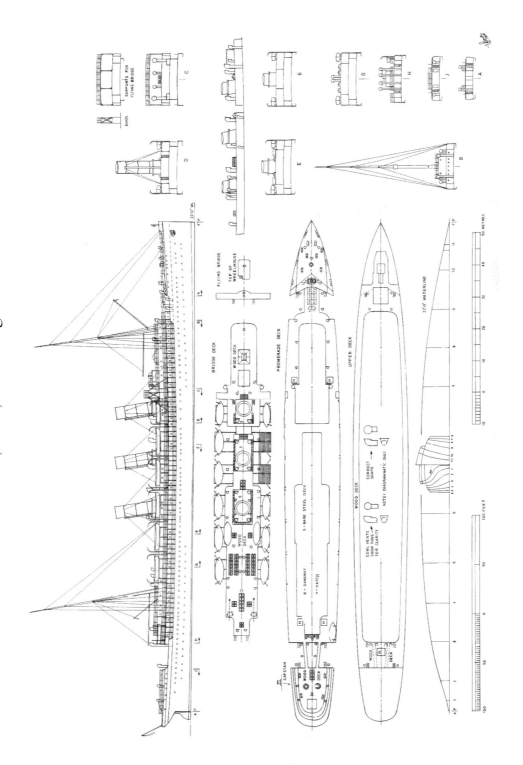

telegraphs. Most photographs of the ship show that the rails round this platform were covered with a canvas dodger. The appearance of the model will be improved if a narrow strip of paper, like a bulwark, is fitted round the edge of the platform; two openings should be left in way of the access ladders. A shallow house, some 8ft (2.5m) high and 2ft (0.6m) deep and providing storage space for – and giving access to – the navigation lights, sat at the bottom of each of the pairs of stanchions supporting the outboard ends of the platform. This house can be represented by a small piece of wood. Diagonal braces were fitted between the stanchions from the top of this house to the underside of the platform. There were also two steadying stays, one running forward and the other aft, from the outboard ends of the platform.

There was a breakwater on the forecastle immediately forward of the windlass, together with a capstan and the usual mooring gear. A low casing with a curved top was found at the after end of the poop.

A 46ft- (14m-) long derrick was mounted on the fore side of the foremast, with a fixed span to the mast, with a 37ft (11.3m) boom (not a cargo derrick) on the after side. The mainmast had a similar boom, but of 56ft (17m) in length. Two 32ft (9.6m) derricks were on the Bridge Deck adjacent to the mainmast (with heel fittings on the deck), which were stowed on the deck when not in use. All cowl ventilators have bell-shaped cowls, which were typical of the period.

Colour Scheme

Hull: black, red below waterline.
Superstructure: white, deckhouses white.
Masts, derricks, booms: buff.
Hatches: buff.
Ventilators: buff, inside cowls red.
Boats and davits: white, light grey covers.
Windlass, winches, capstans: black.
Bollards and fairleads: black.
Decks: all wood planked, but areas of fiddley gratings under funnels black.
Miscellaneous: the four engine room skylights black, other skylights white; breakwater buff; water tank white.

References

There is a fine shipbuilder's model of *Normannia* in the Museum of Transport, Glasgow (see Appendix II, pp205–206) The National Maritime Museum in Greenwich has a rigging plan, GA of all decks and a sheer elevation with a body plan; *Sea Breezes* Volume 59 (September 1985) contains an article on the ship by J H Isherwood in his 'Steamers of the Past' series; *Engineering* (29 August 1890) includes an article 'The New Hamburg-American Twin-Screw steamer *Normannia*', which deals with the construction of the vessel. The machinery was covered in a subsequent article.

The builder's model of *Normannia* in the Museum of Transport, Glasgow.   *Photograph: John Bowen*

25

Oceanic
(1889)

WHITE STAR LINE

Oceanic marked the change from her owners previous policy of speed to the building of ships of large size and moderate speed, with high standards in passenger comfort. Her overall length of 704ft exceeded that of Brunel's *Great Eastern* – hitherto the longest vessel ever built – by some 11ft. She was a fine-looking ship, as testified by her long hull with its sweeping sheer and graceful counter.

She left Liverpool on her maiden voyage to New York on 6 September 1899, and soon settled down on the owners' transatlantic service, where she became a favourite ship. Upon the outbreak of war in 1914 she was immediately taken over by the Admiralty and fitted out as an armed merchant cruiser. Commissioned into the Tenth Cruiser Squadron, her service in this role was tragically short. On 8 September 1914 when patrolling the North West Approaches she went ashore in fog on the Hoevdi Grund reef (the Shaalds) just east of the island of Foula in the Shetlands. Efforts to refloat the ship were put in hand at once, but without success, and the crew were taken off and transferred to the Allan liner *Alsatian*, which was also serving with the Tenth Cruiser Squadron as an AMC.

Three weeks later there was a very severe storm and the vessel broke up and sank in comparatively shallow water. *The Other Titanic* by Simon Martin (see References) gives an admirable account of her loss and of the salvage operation that took place many years later, which succeeded in finding some of her gear and fittings.

Modelling Notes

The heavy bar stem extends some 2ft (0.6m) above the Forecastle Deck and a pair of fairleads is built on to its after side. The Forecastle Deck is planked and there is an additional area of wood sheathing (probably about 4in [10cm] thick) laid on top between the stem and the forward break-

Specification	
Length overall:	704ft 0in (214.5m)
Length bp:	685ft 6in (208.8m)
Breadth mld:	68ft 4in (20.8m)
Load draught:	32ft 4in (9.8m)
Tonnage, gross:	17,274
Machinery:	Two sets 4-cylinder triple expansion engines driving twin screws; 15 boilers, return-type, 12DE and 3SE, 192psi working pressure.
Speed:	19 knots
Passengers, as built:	1700 passengers in three classes

water in way of the capstan and anchor and cable gear. For clarity the forecastle guardrails have been drawn with three bars only, whereas they are in fact six-bar rails and all of round iron. In the openings in the Upper Deck bulwarks each side forward and aft there are three horizontal bars, fitted below the heavy capping rail.

The curtain plate along the edge of the Promenade Deck is about 15in (0.38m) deep, and that on the Boat Deck about 12in (0.3m).

The lifeboat davits are fitted on the outside of the curtain plates, with the davit heel socket fitted on the Promenade Deck curtain plate.

A screen bulkhead the height of the adjacent deckhouse surrounds the ventilation fan units at the base of each funnel. The aftermost boat on each side of the Boat Deck is stowed on deck inside the mainmast shrouds and backstays. For clarity the ratlines have been omitted from the shrouds to all three masts. There are no davits to these two boats.

The foremast is 36in (0.9m) diameter at deck level, the mainmast 33in (0.82m) and the mizzenmast 30in (0.75m). Although the ship was fitted with derricks for handling cargo and baggage, they are not shown on the plan. From photographs it would appear that they were unshipped when at sea. In view of the height of the derrick heel fittings at the masts, the appearance of the vessel was enhanced by this practice. Part of the Boat Deck between the funnels is raised 2ft (0.6m) above the rest of the deck, and this area extends under the deckhouse lying just aft of the elevated compass platform. As this deckhouse is of normal height, it means that the screen bulkhead round the fan units in way of the after funnel is 2ft higher than that round the units at the base of the forward funnel.

The hull can be carved to the level of the Upper Deck, with poop and forecastle being added as solid blocks before the hull sides are added. The shape of the counter is essential. The bulwark and poop should be cut from mounted shaving and fitted by the rebate method.

The long house on the Upper Deck can be made in one piece, but must be well clamped to the hull block while the glue is drying to bond fully with the sheer of the Upper Deck. Alternatively, as deck card will cover the house, two or three small wood screws can be used to secure full adhesion. The two small houses and the three hatches (marked H) should also be fitted at this time. These, as well as the sides of the house, the exposed areas of Upper Deck and the inside of the bulwarks, must be painted before the deck card representing the Promenade Deck is fitted. This card should include two short 'tails' at its after end to form the gangways to the poop.

The forecastle must also be covered by a card, extended as shown to cover the adjacent deckhouse and with a 'tail' for the gangway to the Promenade Deck. The rest of the superstructure and fittings should not present any problems.

Colour Scheme

Hull: black, with golden yellow ribband. The top of this ribband was level with the underside of the teak capping on the Upper Deck bulwark and follows the line of the lower edge of the white sides of the Forecastle and Poop Decks, but it was separated from the white by a narrow black line about 4in (0.1m) wide. The ribband was 6in (0.15m) wide.

Boot topping: red.

Deckhouses: white; lower half of houses on the Upper Deck, including those under the forecastle and poop, mid-brown; there is a 12in- (0.3m-) deep mid-brown kick-

RMS *Oceanic*   *Photograph: author's collection*

Oceanic (1889) White Star Line

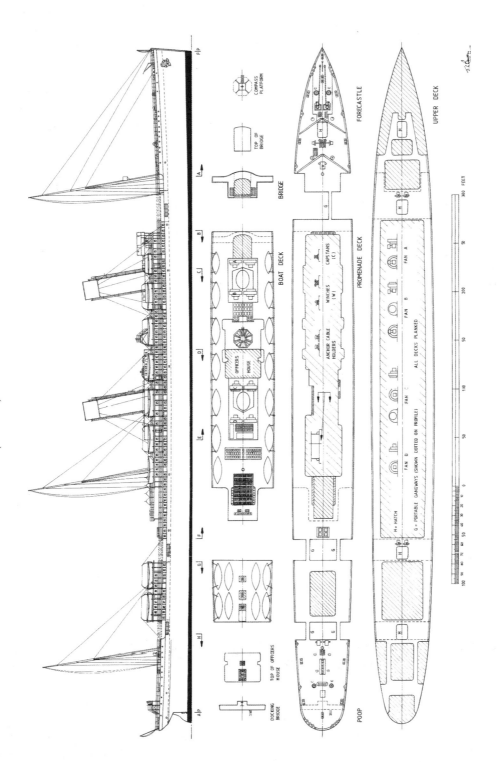

COMPASS PLATFORM

TOP OF BRIDGE

BRIDGE

TOP OF OFFICERS HOUSE

DOCKING BRIDGE

BOAT DECK

OFFICERS' HOUSE

FORECASTLE

ANCHOR CABLE HOLDERS

WINCHES (W)

CAPSTANS (C)

PROMENADE DECK

POOP

UPPER DECK

FAN A

FAN B

FAN C

FAN D

H = HATCH

G = PORTABLE GANGWAYS (SHOWN DOTTED ON PROFILE)

ALL DECKS PLANKED

300 FEET

Oceanic (1889) White Star Line

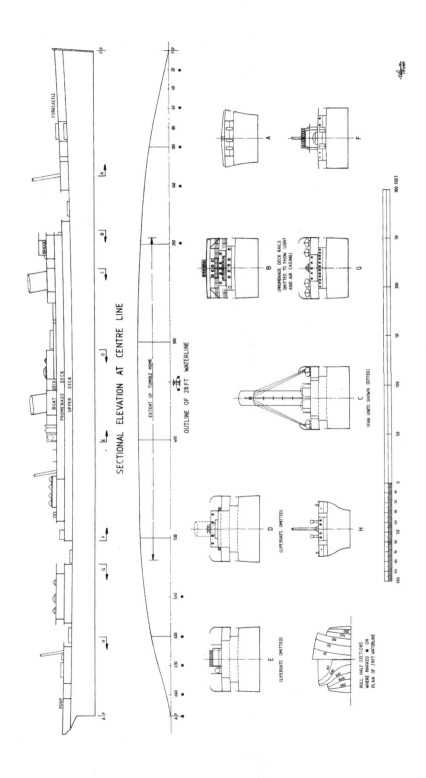

SECTIONAL ELEVATION AT CENTRE LINE

OUTLINE OF 28 FT WATERLINE

EXTENT OF TUMBLE HOME

FORECASTLE

BRIDGE

BOAT DECK
PROMENADE DECK
UPPER DECK

POOP

A

F

B
(PROMENADE DECK RAILS
OMITTED TO SHOW LIGHT
AND AIR CASING)

G

C
(FAN UNITS SHOWN DOTTED)

D
(LIFEBOATS OMITTED)

H

E
(LIFEBOATS OMITTED)

HULL HALF SECTIONS
WHERE MARKED ■ ON
PLAN OF 28 FT WATERLINE

300 FEET

This starboard bow view of *Oceanic* shows some of the bridge front details.   *Photograph: author's collection*

ing strip at the bottom of all other deckhouses; compass platform white.

Skylights: dark brown; engine room skylight has white ends and sides and black top.

Ventilators: white, with red inside cowls; fan units white.

Bollards, fairleads: black.

Anchors, capstans, winches: black.

Anchor cable: white, where visible on deck.

Lifeboats, davits: white, boat covers natural canvas.

Hatches: black.

Masts: ochre-buff; crow's nest on foremast, white.

Ensign staff, jackstaff: white.

Funnels: buff, with black tops; steam pipes to match.

Decks: all planked (teak).

References

Some information about the launching of the ship, its interior arrangements and decoration can be found in: *White Star* by Roy Anderson (Prestcot: Stephenson & Sons, 1964); *The Ismay Line* by Wilton J Oldman (Journal of Commerce & Shipping Telegraph, Liverpool, 1961); *Sea Breezes* Vol X (new series). Constructional notes and launch details can be found in articles in *Engineering* Vol 67 (1899).

Passing references, often with photographs, can be found in practically all of the well-known books about the history of the North Atlantic passenger trade and the ships engaged in this service. *The Other Titanic* by Simon Martin (Newton Abbot: David & Charles, 1980 [ISBN 0 7153 7755 8]) provides the full story of the loss of *Oceanic* and the salvage operation that took place many years later.

26

Oronsay
(1925)

ORIENT LINE

Due to the heavy losses it suffered during World War I, the Orient Line began a major rebuilding programme in the 1920s by ordering five 20,000-ton passenger liners. The orders for four, *Orama*, *Otranto*, *Orford* and *Orontes*, were placed with Vickers Armstrong Ltd, Barrow-in-Furness, with that for the fifth vessel going to John Brown & Co Ltd, Clydebank, Scotland (Yard No 500). All five ships were similar in appearance, although there were some minor differences. *Orontes*, the last to be completed (in 1930), was given a rolled-plate (soft-nosed) stem in place of the bar stem of the others. They were all strong, powerful-looking vessels, with their black hulls and white superstructure surmounted by two tall, nicely raked, cowl-topped, buff (yellow-ochre) funnels, surrounded by several large cowl ventilators. The ships were designed to carry only first- and third-class passengers.

Oronsay, the second ship to be completed, was launched on 16 January 1924 and completed in January 1925. She sailed on her maiden voyage on the Orient Line's UK to Australia service on 7 February 1925, and remained on that route until the outbreak of World War II. She was requisitioned early in 1940 for use as a troop transport and served in this capacity until early in October 1942, when she was sunk off the west coast of Africa by an Italian submarine, fortunately with the loss of only five lives.

Modelling Notes

When looking at the elevations it is clear that there are several ways in which the basic hull block might be made. Probably the best way is to make it to the level of the forecastle (D) deck, then cut down to E Deck level in way of the well forward and again at the after end. The opening each side aft in way of F deck can be made as a shallow slot, if preferred, instead of cutting away to F Deck level. After painting the interior of the slot, the opening should be fitted with

Specification	
Length overall:	658ft 6in (200.71m)
Length bp:	630ft 0in (192.02m)
Breadth mld:	75ft 0in (22.86m)
Draught:	28ft 6in (8.69m)
Tonnage, gross:	20,001 tons
Machinery:	geared turbines, 20,000 shp, twin screw
Speed:	20 knots
Passengers, as built:	600 first class, 1200 third

a bulwark by the rebate method, the deck stanchions being glued to the inside of the bulwark and trimmed to length before it is fitted.

The superstructure is formed by a build-up of a series of deckhouses and deck cards. The heights of the houses can be determined from the sectional profile. Note that there is an area of raised deck at the forward end of the Boat Deck, and that the Promenade and Boat Decks are increased in breadth to 79ft 0in (24m).

On each side of the ship, abreast the foremast, a 25ft (7.6m) lifeboat is stowed inside a 28ft (8.5m) lifeboat. Gravity davits are fitted to handle the boats, the inboard end of each trackway being supported by an A-frame. On the Boat Deck, the forward boat each side is stowed on deck and handled by quadrant davits. The aftermost boat each side on this deck is a motor boat, stowed on gravity davits. The remaining boats each side on this deck are 28ft, each with a 25ft boat stowed inside, again handled by gravity davits with trackways supported at the inboard end by an A-frame. On the After Boat Platform there is a 28ft (8.4m) boat with a 28ft collapsible stowed on deck underneath, both served by quadrant davits. Inboard of these, each side, is a similar pair of boats. Between them, on the centre line, a single collapsible is stowed on a trolley set on rails running athwartship to either side of the deck. On the cross-sections on the plans, one boat and its cradle has been omitted on the opposite side for clarity.

As well as the very large cowl ventilators in way of the funnels (note that four of these are set on cranked trunking) and the slightly smaller ones grouped on the boiler and engine casings and adjacent houses, there are a considerable number of smaller cowl ventilators throughout the ship, which are visible in photographs of the five liners. There are several very small cowl ventilators set close to the edge of the forecastle deck each side, while those along each side of the Promenade Deck are larger.

Colour Scheme

Hull: black to level of the top of the bulwark to the well deck forward, white above; boot topping green.
Superstructure: white, inside of bulwarks white; wheelhouse, Navigating Bridge bulwark and wing cabs mahogany.

Masts, mast tables, derrick posts, derricks: red-brown.
Lifeboats and davits: white, covers grey.
Ventilators: large cowl ventilators in way of funnels, and those on the casings abaft the after funnel, yellow-ochre; elsewhere white; inside of all cowls red.
Windlass, winches, capstans, bollards, hatches: as funnels.
Funnels: yellow-ochre, with black cowls.
Decks: all wood planked; top of houses in way of funnels, and top of after deckhouse on Boat Deck, black.
Skylights: white.

References

Glasgow University Business Records Centre holds general arrangement plans of the ship, plus a number of others; the Scottish Record Office in Edinburgh has two broadside photographs (one port, one starboard) of the ship as completed – reference nos UCS1/412-2 and UCS1/412-3 – and may have others; *Shipbuilding & Shipping Record* (21 August 1924) contains an article on *Oceanic's* launch. See Appendix II, pp205–206, for contact details.

Articles on the sister ships can also be found, most of which provide small-scale completion and general arrangement plans. These drawings are detailed although the arrangement of the house tops in plan view is not included,

The *Oronsay* (1925)   *Photograph: author's collection*

Oronsay (1925) Orient Line

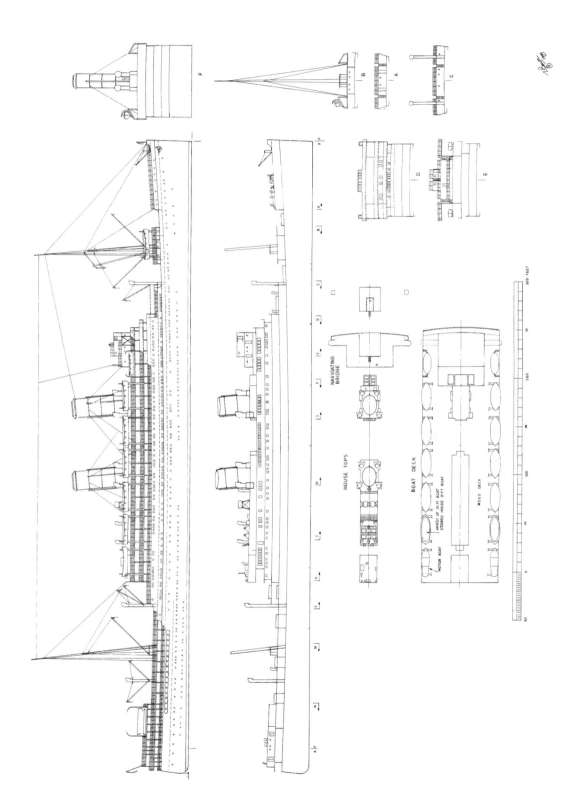

NAVIGATING BRIDGE

HOUSE TOPS

BOAT DECK

WOOD DECK

MOTOR BOAT

PARROT OF 25 FT BOAT STOWED INSIDE 31 FT BOAT

Oronsay (1925) Orient Line

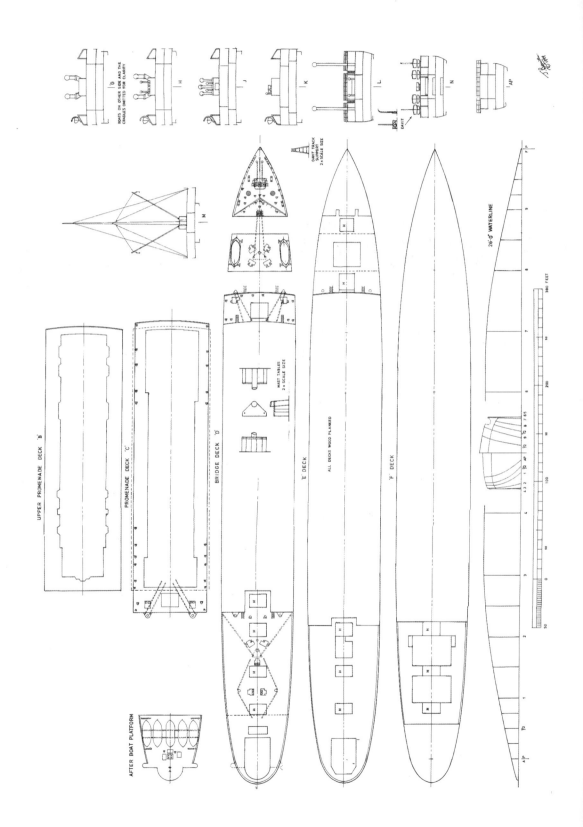

As this photograph of the *Oronsay's* sister ship *Otranto* shows, the five sister ships were very similar in overall appearance.

Photograph: author's collection

and small details such as ventilators are generally missing from the deck plans: *Otranto – Shipbuilding & Shipping Record* (28 January 1926); *Orford – Shipbuilding & Shipping Record* (19 April 1928); *Orama – The Shipbuilder* (January 1928); *Orontes – The Shipbuilder* (January 1930).

For general reading about the Orient Line: *Ships of the Orient Line* by Neil McCart (Patrick Stephens, 1987 [ISBN 0-85059-891-5]); *ORIGINS, Orient & Oriana* by Charles F Morris (Teredo Books Ltd, 1980 [ISBN 0-903662-07-8]), which mainly contains the design and construction of the 1960 *Oriana* but also includes a general history of the line and its ships.

27

Otaio
(1930)

NEW ZEALAND SHIPPING COMPANY LIMITED

Otaio was the first of three large refrigerated cargo ships completed in 1930–31 for the New Zealand Shipping Company's UK to Australia and New Zealand service. She was torpedoed and sunk on 28 August 1941 in the North Atlantic when part of an outward-bound convoy. Her sister ship *Opawa* was torpedoed and sunk early in 1942 in the Atlantic when homeward bound from New Zealand. The third ship of the trio, *Orari*, was damaged by a torpedo in December 1940 but managed to reach the Clyde where, after the cargo had been discharged, she was repaired. In June 1942 she made headline news when, after enduring heavy air attacks and then striking a mine half a mile from her destination, she reached Malta, one of only two vessels from the six-ship convoy to survive and reach the

Specification	
Length overall:	490ft 0in (149.35m)
Length bp:	470ft 0in (143.25m)
Breadth, mld:	67ft 4in (20.52m)
Draught:	32ft 3in (9.8m)
Tonnage, gross:	10,048
Machinery:	Doxford diesel engines, 400bhp; twin screw
Speed:	16 knots

Otaio as completed.

Photograph: author's collection

Otaio as completed.

beleagured island with essential supplies. After local repairs she returned to the UK and continued in service until 1953–4 when she was laid up. In 1958 she was sold to new owners in Palermo (Sicily) and renamed *Capo Bianco* and was broken up in Italy in 1971.

Otaio was built by Vickers, Armstrong & Co Ltd, Barrow-in-Furness, while *Opawa* and *Orari* were built by Alexander Stephen & Son Ltd at Linthouse in Glasgow. All three ships followed the same basic principles, but there were minor differences introduced by the two builders. For example, the two Stephen's ships had cowl tops fitted to the pair of derrick posts immediately abaft the superstructure in place of the mushroom tops.

With a slightly raked bar stem, cruiser stern, midship accommodation block and an impressive outfit of cargo-handling equipment, they were fine-looking ships that set the pattern for big refrigerated cargo vessels put into service on the UK to Australia and New Zealand run by several owners in the ensuing years.

Modelling Notes

As with other vessels of a similar hull form, the hull can be made to the level of the Poop, Bridge and Forecastle Decks then cut down forward and aft to the Upper Deck to form the two wells (the sides of which are enclosed by bulwarks). These can be prepared from paper-mounted shavings,

remembering to cut the freeing port openings before fitting in place.

The superstructure is made up of five separate houses, their overall height being reduced by the thickness of the card used to form the overhanging decks. There is a bulwark along each side of the Upper Deck for the length of the midship structure, one across the fore end of both Promenade Deck and Boat Deck and another along each side of these decks to a point just beyond the forward lifeboat. The lifeboats are carried on gravity type davits.

Of the four winch houses of the Forecastle, Bridge and Poop Decks three have the same general shape in plan view, though one is shorter transversely than the other two; the fourth, the one in way of the foremast, is slightly different. The sketch on the plan shows how the top outboard corners of the first three houses are snapped away. All four have the same straight-line 'bay' windows. It is better to add these as separate pieces, cut from a length of lime or other wood finished so that its end cross section is the shape of the 'bay' windows as seen from above. From this strip cut off pieces slightly longer than the depth of the house and glue them in place. When dry trim away the surplus wood flush with the top and bottom of the house. It is easier, and quicker, to do this and gives a better finish. These houses contain all the winch motors and control gear, with only the barrel and warping ends being fitted outside. The cargo hatches have

Otaio (1930) New Zealand Shipping Company Limited

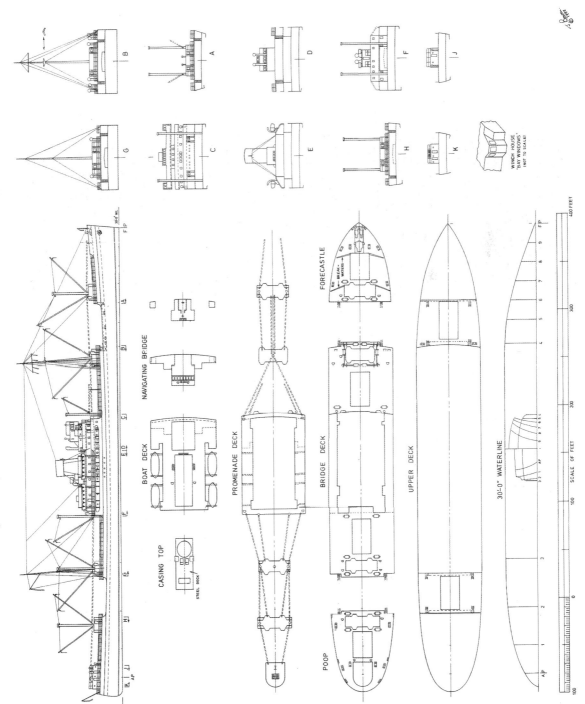

Otaio's sister ship *Orari* in her post-war colour scheme. She now carries a radar mast and scanner on top of the wheelhouse.

Photograph: author's collection

peaked transverse coamings and are covered with tarpaulins.

Colour Scheme

Hull: black, to level of top of well deck bulwarks, white above, including forecastle and Bridge Deck bulwarks; boot topping red; narrow white dividing ribband; ends of forecastle, long bridge house and poop, lower half mid-grey, upper half white.

Superstructure: white, except house on Bridge Deck, top on Poop Deck and four winch houses, lower half mid-grey, upper half white.

Hatches: coamings mid-grey, tops green.

Masts, derrick posts, derricks: red brown (Humbrol 100).

Lifeboats and davits: white, boat covers green.

Ventilators: white, inside cowls red; two mushroom ventilators abaft funnel as funnel colour.

Windlass: mid grey.

Winches: mid grey.

Bollards, fairleads: black.

Funnel: pale cream/yellow (Humbrol 69 with some white added).

Miscellaneous: skylights white, water tanks abaft funnel as funnel colour.

References

The technical journal *The Motor Ship* (January 1931) contains an article and small-scale general-arrangement (GA) plan of the ship; *Sea Breezes* volume 62 (October 1988) includes an article by B M Leek about the ship in his series 'These Splendid Ships'.

28

Politician or 'The Whisky Ship' (1923)

T & G HARRISON LTD

In 1947 Compton Mackenzie wrote a book entitled *Whisky Galore*, which was subsequently made into a film. The incident that inspired his humorous story of the clandestine activities around a ship with a cargo of whisky wrecked close to a remote island off the Scottish West Coast during the war, occurred in February 1941. T & J Harrison's steamer *Politician*, outward bound from Liverpool for the West Indies with a general cargo, which included the equivalent of 22,000 cases or 264,000 bottles of Scotch whisky, ran aground in heavy weather in the Sound of Eriskay in the Outer Hebrides (off the north-west coast of Scotland). Some of the local populace soon commandeered the cargo, primarily the whisky, but their foray was brief for HM Customs took steps to stop their activities.

Most of the cargo, including a large proportion of the whisky, was salvaged in 1941. The ship was then cut in two, the fore part towed away and the after end cut down to low water level and the remains demolished by explosives.

The *Politician* was an interesting vessel in other ways. She was built for the Furness Withy group at the shipyard established by Lord Furness in 1918 at Haverton Hill-on-Tees (on the north-east coast of England) to build tonnage for the group. Launched as the *London Merchant* in 1923, she was one of six similar single-screw cargo ships ordered for the owners' UK to USA services.

The lines of the vessel were on a modified straight-frame principle with rounded bilges. The stern was of a conical form and the hull without sheer. The advantage of this hull form lay in the fact that virtually the whole of the shell plating could be developed on the mould loft floor, thereby eliminating the more customary, but time consuming, practice of making templates for the shell plates from the ship as she lay in frame on the building berth. Moreover, furnacing

Specification	
Length overall:	471ft 6in (143.71m)
Length bp:	450ft 0in (137.16m)
Breadth:	58ft 0in (17.68m)
Draught:	30ft 2in (9.19m)
Tonnage, gross:	7896
Machinery:	two single reduction steam turbines, 5000dhp; single screw
Speed:	14½ knots

of shaped plates was almost eliminated.

Another design feature was the concentration of all accommodation within a short midship structure. Years later in 1928 the Canadian Pacific Company adopted a similar layout for their *Beaver* class. In fact their overall appearance was markedly similar to *London Merchant* in many respects, although the hull had sheer and a cruiser stern. It is interesting to note that they retained the short superstructure in their new post-World War II *Beaver*-class cargo ships.

In 1930 the *London Merchant*, along with several of her sisters, was laid up in the river Blackwater in Essex. In 1935 she was bought by T & J Harrison, together with her sister ships *London Mariner*, *London Commerce* and *London Shipper*. The vessels were renamed *Politician*, *Craftsman*, *Collegian* and *Statesman* respectively. *Politician*, as mentioned earlier, was lost on Eriskay and of the other three, *Craftsman* and *Statesman* became war losses and *Collegian* was scrapped at Milford Haven in 1947.

Politician

The conical shape of the stern can be seen in this photograph.

Photographs: author's collection

Politician (1923) T & G Harrison Ltd

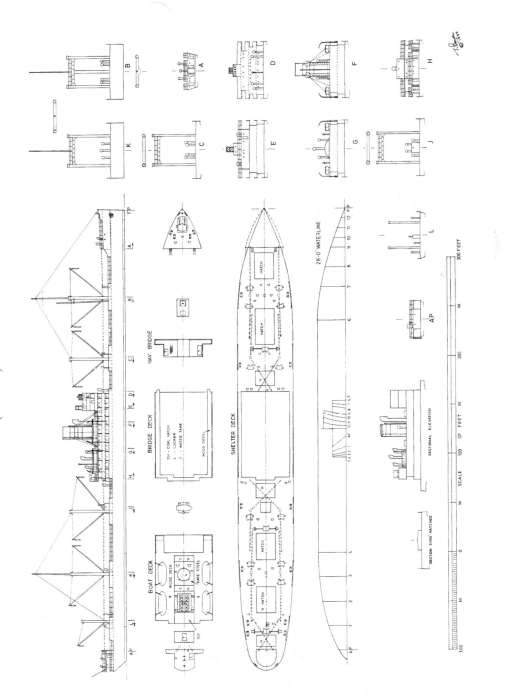

Modelling Notes

As the hull is without sheer it can be formed from a rectangular strip of wood, such as lime, 0.58in wide x 0.28in deep (about 15mm x 7mm) i.e. the depth from the Shelter Deck to the load waterline. If the model is to be set in a sea, then the thickness of the strip should be increased by a suitable amount. Once the top surface of the hull has been sanded smooth, the outline of the Shelter Deck marked on the top and that of the waterline marked on the underside (but before the hull is shaped), the forecastle can be added as a separate block. The Forecastle Deck has a slight sheer, so the thickness of the block must be at least equal to the height of the fore end of the forecastle, though it does not matter if it is more. The after end of this block must be finished square and vertical before being glued and dowelled in place, care being taken to see that its after end is exactly on the line of the break of the forecastle (i.e. line of the forecastle bulkhead) and square to the centre line of the ship. Once the glue has set the top surface of the block can be pared away down to the line of the sheer of the Forecastle Deck. When this has been done the hull can be carved to shape; note that the bow has an easy and gently pronounced flare.

The rest of the model should not present any undue difficulties, since all houses are rectangular and all masts vertical.

Colour Scheme

Hull: black above waterline, to level of Shelter Deck; boot topping salmon pink; sides of forecastle and bulwarks white.
Superstructure: white, but lower half of forecastle bulkhead and lower half of the sides and ends of all deckhouses (other than those forming the front of the superstructure), mast brown.
Hatches: coamings mast brown, tops black.
Windlass, winches: black.
Bollards, fairleads: black.
Masts, derrick posts, derricks: masts brown (Humbrol 133 Satin Brown is about the nearest shade).
Lifeboats, davits: white, grey covers to boats.
Ventilators: white, but those on the Boat Deck black; inside of all cowls red.
Funnel: black, with red/white/red bands.
Lockers etc: white.

References

Whisky Galore by Compton Mackenzie (London: Penguin Books, 1947 [ISBN 0 14 001220 6]); *Polly* by Roger Hutchinson (Edinburgh, Scotland: Mainstream Publishing, 1990 [ISBN 1-85158-335-1]), tells for the first time the true story of the *Politician* (or *Polly* as she was known locally) – including the stranding, salvage and demise, what really happened to the cargo and the part played by HM Customs and others – and is a fascinating read.

29

Salween (1938)

P HENDERSON & CO LTD

The geared turbine steamer *Salween* was completed for the British & Burmese Steam Navigation Company (P Henderson & Co, better known as 'Paddy Henderson') by William Denny & Brothers Limited, at Dumbarton in 1938 (Yard No 1307). Denny had delivered an almost identical sister ship *Prome* (Yard No 1295) the previous year. They were the last two passenger ships ordered by Henderson for their UK to Burma service, a route that they and their friendly rivals, the Bibby Line, dominated for many decades. During World War II *Salween* was used as a troopship while *Prome* served as a mine depot ship. Once hostilities had ceased both ships resumed the Rangoon service. They were withdrawn in 1962, *Salween* going to shipbreakers in Hong Kong and *Prome* to scrappers in Bruges, Belgium.

Slightly smaller than their Bibby counterparts, they were smart, good-looking ships. As completed, *Prome* was easy to identify because of her two tall cowl ventilators immediately forward of the funnel and the white bulwark round the standard compass on top of the wheelhouse.

Modelling Notes

The plan is for the ship as built. The hull is of a typical three-island type and can be made either by cutting the sheer to the top of the poop, bridge and forecastle, and cutting out the two wells, or by cutting to the line of the Upper Deck and adding pieces, with the appropriate end faces fully finished, to form the poop, bridge and forecastle. In either case, once the hull has been fully shaped, paper-mounted shavings will have to be cut and fitted to form the well deck bulwarks, with another short bulwark at the stem head.

The superstructure is made up of a number of rectangular houses with deck cards in between to form the overhanging deck, their thickness being equal to the depth of the curtain plates, about 12in (0.3m). The bulwark along the side of the Bridge Deck is best added by the rebate

Specification

Length overall:	460ft 6in (140.36m)
Length bp:	439ft 3in (133.88m)
Breadth:	59ft 0in (17.98m)
Draught:	27ft 0in (8.23m)
Tonnage, gross:	7063 tons
Machinery:	geared turbine, single screw
Speed:	14 knots

method because of its length. As the corners of the decks are square, the bulwarks across the front of the superstructure and each side between the Promenade and Boat Decks can be added separately. There is a large open verandah at the after end of the Promenade Deck.

Cowl ventilators are quite a feature of the ship, and there are two fan units by the funnel. On the Boat Deck, forward of the engine room skylight, are two small cylindrical water tanks. The heel fittings of the derricks on each mast are stepped on a robust table, the outboard ends of which are supported by a single pillar. The heel fitting of the heavy derrick at the foremast is on deck. Each mast is fitted with an outrigger and there is a small signal yard on the foremast and a short gaff on the mainmast. The upper part of the mainmast is painted black from a point just below the outrigger to the top.

Colour Scheme

Hull: black to level of poop, bridge and forecastle, and including stem bulwark: boot topping pink; narrow white dividing ribband between boot top and hull black; ends of poop, bridge and forecastle white; inside of well deck

Salween almost fully loaded.

The sister ship *Prome* can be distinguished by the two tall ventilators just forward of the funnel, and by the white bulwark round the standard compass on top of the wheelhouse.

Photographs: K Byass

Salween (1938) P Henderson & Co Ltd

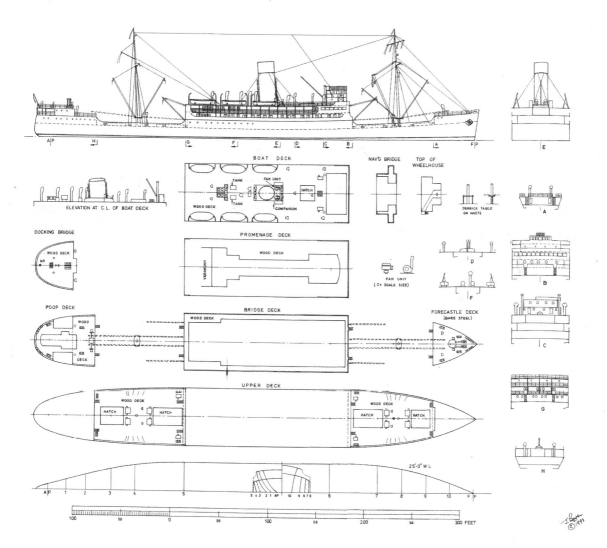

ELEVATION AT C.L. OF BOAT DECK

BOAT DECK

TANK
FAN UNIT
WOOD DECK
TANK
COMPANION
HATCH

NAV'G BRIDGE

TOP OF WHEELHOUSE

DERRICK TABLE ON MASTS

A

DOCKING BRIDGE

WOOD DECK

PROMENADE DECK

WOOD DECK

VERANDAH

FAN UNIT
(2x SCALE SIZE)

D

F

B

POOP DECK

WOOD

DECK

BRIDGE DECK

WOOD DECK

FORECASTLE DECK
(BARE STEEL)

D

D

C

UPPER DECK

WOOD DECK

HATCH   HATCH

WOOD DECK

HATCH   HATCH

G

25'-0" W L

AP 1 2 3 4 5   5 4 3 2 1 AP 10 9 8 7 6   6   7   8   9   10   FP

H

100   50   0   50   100   50   200   50   300 FEET

bulwarks light grey.

Superstructure: white, inside of bulwarks white.

Masts, derricks posts, derricks: medium grey, but derrick posts abaft bridge white.

Hatches: coamings and covers medium grey.

Lifeboats, davits: white, grey canvas covers.

Ventilators: light grey, inside of cowls red.

Windlass, winches: medium grey.

Bollards, fairleads: black.

Funnel: black.

Decks: wood planked, but forecastle is bare steel (dark red oxide).

Miscellaneous: skylights teak, engine room skylight white; top of boiler casing in way of funnel black; water tanks white; three tall, thin funnels on the poop deck grey.

References

The National Maritime Museum in Greenwich holds outboard profile and GA plans of all decks for both ships, a midship section and painting profile for *Prome*, plus a number of photographs of both ships (see Appendix II, pp205–206).

The full history of P Henderson & Company is told in *Paddy Henderson* by Dorothy Laird (Glasgow: George Outram & Co, 1961).

30

Sarpedon
(1923)

BLUE FUNNEL LINE

After the end of World War I there was a big demand for passages to the Far East, so the Blue Funnel Line fitted several of its cargo ships with limited accommodation for passengers. This proved to be very successful, and the company ordered four passenger–cargo steamers with accommodation for 135–155 passengers for their Liverpool to Far East service. *Sarpedon* was completed by Cammell Laird, Birkenhead in 1923, *Patroclus* by Scotts Shipbuilding & Engineering Co Ltd, Greenock, in 1923, with *Hector* coming from the same yard the following year, while *Antenor* was built by Palmers Shipbuilding Co Ltd at Jarrow in 1925. All were fine, sturdy vessels, with that typical 'Blue Funnel' appearance of good sheer, raked stem, counter stern, and vertical masts and funnel.

There were some minor differences between the four ships. *Sarpedon* was the only one to carry a lifeboat on each side of the Upper Boat Deck and *Hector* and *Antenor* did not have derrick posts at the after end of the Boat Deck.

Patroclus became an AMC (Armed Merchant Cruiser) in September 1939, but was bombed and sunk in 1940. *Hector* was also converted to an AMC in 1940 and was bombed and sunk in Colombo harbour in 1942. *Antenor* served throughout the war as a troopship, and after a refit returned to her owner's service to the Far East and Australia. *Sarpedon* remained with her owners throughout the war and following a refit she joined *Antenor* on the Far East/Australia run. She was broken up at Newport, South Wales in 1953, with *Antenor* being scrapped at Blyth in Northumberland the same year.

Modelling Notes

There are several points to keep in mind when building this model. Accuracy in cutting the sheer is all-important, for it is a marked characteristic of most Blue Funnel ships. Masts, funnel and so on are vertical, though if they seem to be lean-

Specification	
Length overall:	516ft 6in (157.4m)
Length bp:	490ft 9in (149.6m)
Breadth mld:	62ft 0in (18.9m)
Draught:	30ft 0in (9.1m)
Tonnage, gross:	11,400 tons
Machinery:	geared turbines, 7500 shp, twin screw
Speed:	15 knots
Passengers:	135 first class

ing slightly forward when the model is viewed from the side, they can be given a very, very (emphasis on the very, very) small rake aft. There are two ways of making the hull: by carving it to the level of the Upper Deck and adding the poop, bridge (midship house) and forecastle as separate pieces, remembering to finish the inboard ends of each before fitting in place; or carving to the level of the poop, bridge and forecastle and then cutting away the two wells to the level of the Upper Deck. In each case the well deck bulwarks, cut from mounted shavings, can be fitted by the rebate method.

When working on the superstructure great care must be taken to get the height of deckhouses, particularly those forming the very tall bridge structure, exactly right, otherwise it will look unbalanced.

As mentioned already, the funnel, masts and derrick posts are vertical. The derricks on the cowl-topped derrick posts have fixed spans, thus these derricks are always in the working position. The remainder stow as indicated. The heavy

The *Sarpedon*   *Photograph: author's collection*

derrick on the after side of the foremast is stowed vertically against the mast with its heel fitting on the deck. The centre line derrick on the fore side of the foremast, and those on the fore-and-aft side of the mainmast, stow vertically against their masts with their heel fittings on the mast tables. The heel fittings of the wing derricks are also on the mast tables.

The lifeboats port and starboard on the poop are stowed on pedestals with their keels level with the top of the guardrails. The whole boat is inside the edge of the deck. Their radial-type davits are set in pedestals on the deck. The midship boats are stowed on chocks on the deck, but their radial davits pass through the deck to a heel fitting on the deck below. Note that the davits are painted black, which is another feature of many Blue Funnel ships.

Colour Scheme

Hull: black to the level of the top of the well deck bulwarks; sides of the forecastle, bridge and poop white; boot topping pink.

Superstructure, deckhouses: white; wheelhouse mahogany.

Masts, derrick posts, derricks: golden brown (use Humbrol 62); the two derrick posts in front of the super-structure, and the two at the after end of the Boat Deck, white; inside of cowls light blue (as funnel colour).

Lifeboats: white, covers light grey; davits black above deck level, white below.

Hatches: black.

Windlass, winches: black.

Bollards, fairleads: black.

Ventilators: on engine and boiler casing black, elsewhere white; inside of cowls pale blue (as funnel).

Decks: forecastle, well decks and area in way of funnel, which are bare steel, black; poop and superstructure decks wood planked.

Funnel: pale blue, black top.

Miscellaneous: fiddley gratings, engine room skylight black.

References

Shipbuilding & Shipping Record (8 February 1923) contains a short article covering the launch of the ship; *Sea Breezes* Volume 60 No 492, (December 1986) includes an article on the ship by J H Isherwood in his 'Steamers of the Past' series; Cammell Laird Archives (held by Wirral Museum, Birkenhead) have a 1/384-scale early outline GA drawing, but it is only moderately detailed (see Appendix II, pp205–206).

Stavangerfjord (1918) Norwegian America Line

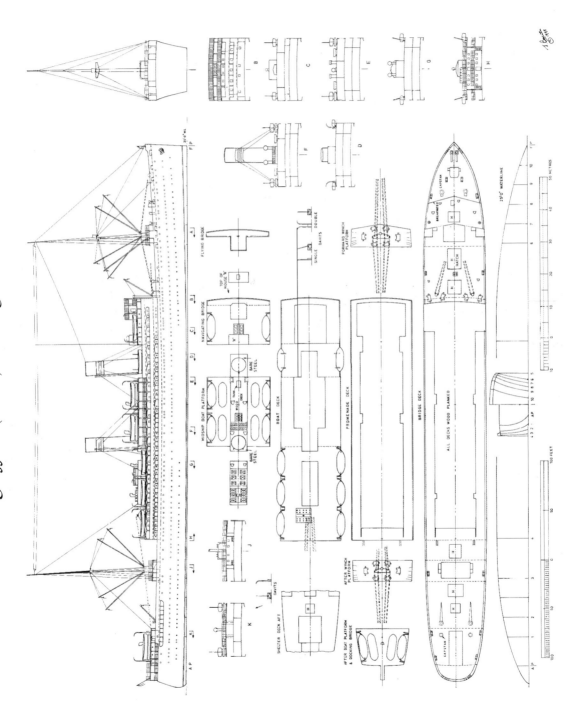

on deck inboard of each of these six boats.

Both masts were fitted with outriggers of similar size, as shown in the section at A. The top part of the mainmast was painted black.

Colour Scheme

Hull: light grey above the waterline to the top of the Bridge Deck bulwark, red below the waterline; narrow white ribband at waterline dividing the grey and red.

Superstructure: white, inside of bulwarks white; Navigating Bridge and Flying Bridge bulwarks mahogany. See note above about their curtain plates.

Deckhouses: white.

Masts, derricks: light buff; mainmast from outrigger to the top, black.

Windlass, winches: dark grey.

Hatches: light grey.

Lifeboats, davits: white, light grey covers to boats without side tabs; boats have brown gunwale strake.

Ventilators: those adjacent to funnels deep cream, as funnel colour, elsewhere white; all cowls red inside.

Funnels: deep cream with red, white, blue, white, red bands (Norwegian national colours).

Decks: all wood planked; bare steel in way of funnels dark grey.

Miscellaneous: skylights, water tanks, white.

Note: as completed the ship left the builder's yard with the Norwegian colours painted on each side abreast the masts. These comprised vertical red/white/blue/white/red stripes running from the level of the Bridge Deck down to about 2ft above the lowest row of portholes. The red (outer) stripes appear to be about 4ft (1.2m) wide and the others about half this width. The ship's name was in large black capital letters about 6ft (2.0m) high set centrally between the first and second rows (from the Bridge Deck down) of portholes, and spread over a length of about 100ft (30.0m) amidships (i.e. from funnel to funnel). These neutrality markings were removed when hostilities ceased.

References

The Norsk Sjofartsmuseum (Oslo, Norway) published a history of the Line under the title *Amerikabatene* by Bard Kolliveit in 1984 (Norwegian text with English summary); *Sea Breezes* Volume 54, No 411 (March 1980) contains a detailed article about the ship by J H Isherwood in his 'Steamers of the past' series; The Birkenhead Library has a small-scale rigging and GA plan of the ship in its Cammell Laird collection, Skyfotos (see Appendix II, pp205–206) has a port broadside aerial photograph of the ship taken in the late 1950s/early 1960s.

APPENDIX I

RMS *Titanic* and *Queen Mary*

Because of their popularity as model subjects (and for the benefit of those who do not have access to the earlier work, *Miniature Merchant Ships*, which features them in depth) the plans of the above two ships and their essential data and colour details have been included in this volume. As the two ships most intimately connected with the *Titanic* disaster – the *Californian* and the *Carpathia* – are featured in Part II, *Titanic* afficionados have all three ships together.

RMS *Titanic* (1912)

WHITE STAR LINE

The *Titanic* was completed in 1912 by Harland & Wolff Ltd, Belfast, for the White Star Line.

Colour Scheme

Hull: black to a level 10in below the top of the Shelter Deck bulwark; narrow (10in) yellow ribband all round hull, the top edge of which is level with the top of the Shelter Deck bulwark; white above the ribband; boot topping red.

Superstructure: white, deckhouses white, but lower half of the houses on the Shelter Deck aft under the Poop brown; tops of houses on the Boat Deck in way of the funnels, black.

Masts, derricks: mid brown.

Ventilators and ventilator units: white, inside cowls red.

Lifeboats, davits: white, sheerstrake on boats mahogany, covers off-white canvas.

Cargo cranes: white.

Cable lifters, anchors, capstans, bollards, fairleads, winches: black.

Hatches: light grey.

Decks: wood planked.

References

A special issue of *The Shipbuilder* (1911) is available as a facsimile reprint by Patrick Stephens Ltd (1970, 1983, 1988); *Engineering* (28 May 1912) article on launch of ship. Note: both the above carry reproductions of the small-scale design plans mentioned earlier.

Specification

Length overall:	882ft 9in (269.04m)
Registered length:	852ft 6in* (259.82m)
Length bp:	850ft 0in (259.06m)
Breadth mld:	92ft 0in (28.04m)
Breadth on Promenade and Boat Decks:	
	94ft 0in (28.64m)
Draught, load:	34ft 0in (10.36m)
Tonnage, gross:	46,328 tons
Machinery:	two 4-cyl triple expansion engines 30,000ihp; one low-pressure turbine 6000shp, triple screw
Speed:	21 knots

* This is the length from the fore part of the stem under the bowsprit (i.e. top of stem) to the aft side of the head of the stern post as entered on the ship's Certificate of Registry, which is made out at the time of her completion. The between perpendiculars (bp) length is taken from the fore side of the stem to the after side of the sternpost (or centre of rudder stock when there is no sternpost) at the summer load line. Any difference between the two sets of figures will be due to stem rake.

Titanic (1912) White Star Line

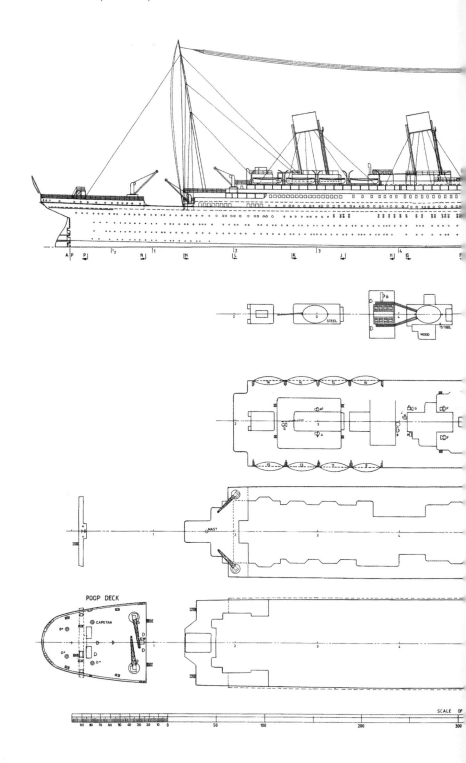

POOP DECK

CAPSTAN

SCALE OF

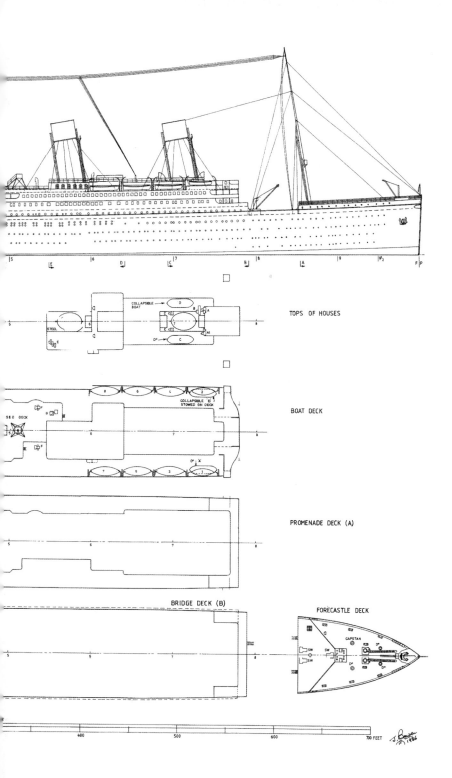

TOPS OF HOUSES

BOAT DECK

PROMENADE DECK (A)

BRIDGE DECK (B)

FORECASTLE DECK

Titanic (1912) White Star Line

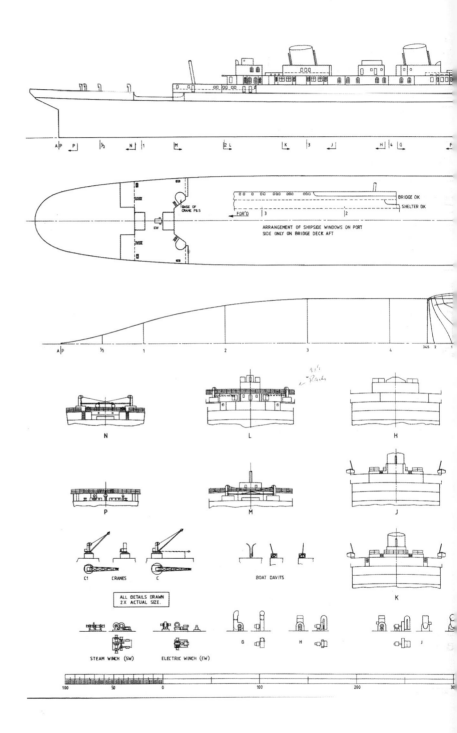

ALL DETAILS DRAWN
2X ACTUAL SIZE.

STEAM WINCH (SW)   ELECTRIC WINCH (EW)

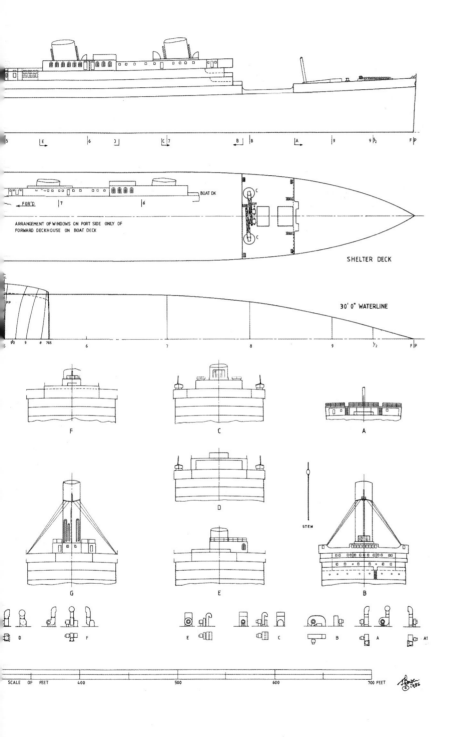

BOAT DK

FOR'D   7   6

ARRANGEMENT OF WINDOWS ON PORT SIDE ONLY OF
FORWARD DECKHOUSE ON BOAT DECK

SHELTER DECK

30' 0" WATERLINE

F   C   A

D

G   E   B

STEM

D   F

E   C   B   A   A1

SCALE OF FEET   400   500   600   700 FEET

RMS *Titanic*

Over the years numerous books have been published, covering every aspect of the tragedy and its aftermath: *RMS Titanic – 75 Years of Legend* by David Hutchings (Kingfisher Railway Productions, 1987 [ISBN 0-946184-29-1]); *Titanic* by Leo Marriott (PRC Publishing Ltd, 1998 [ISBN 1-85648-433-5]); *Anatomy of the Titanic* by Tom McCluskie (PRC Publishing Ltd, 1998 [ISBN 1-85648-482-3]); *Titanic & Her Sisters Olympic and Britannic* by Tom McCluskie, Michael Sharpe and Leo Marriott (PRC Publishing Ltd, 1998 [ISBN 0-868102-612-7]) [note that quite a lot of the material in the first two PRC books is contained in this last volume]; *Titanic – Triumph and Tragedy* by John P Eaton & Charles Haas (Patrick Stephens Ltd, 1968 [ISBN 0-85059-775-7]); *The Birth of the Titanic* by Michael McCaughan (The Blackstaff Press: Belfast, Northern Ireland, 1998 [ISBN 0-85640-631-7]).

APPENDIX I

—

Queen Mary (1936)

—

CUNARD WHITE STAR LINE

The world-famous liner *Queen Mary* (Yard No 534) was built by John Brown & Co Ltd at Clydebank, Scotland in 1936. She is now permanently moored at Long Beach, California, USA, as a convention centre and museum.

Colour Scheme

Hull: black to level of A Deck, red below, with narrow white dividing line.
Superstructure: white.
Masts, derricks: golden brown (Humbrol 62).
Ventilators: white, inside cowls red.
Lifeboats, davits: white, boat covers light grey (Humbrol 64).
Boat winches: white.

Specification

Length overall:	1019ft 6in (310.74m)
Length bp:	965ft 0in (294.13m)
Breadth mld:	118ft 0in (35.97m)
Draught:	38ft 10in (11.84m)
Tonnage, gross:	81,237 tons
Machinery:	turbines 212,000 shp; quadruple screw.
Speed:	28.5 knots

Queen Mary nearing completion in her builder's fitting out basin at Clydebank.

Photograph: author's collection

Queen Mary (1936) Cunard White Star Line

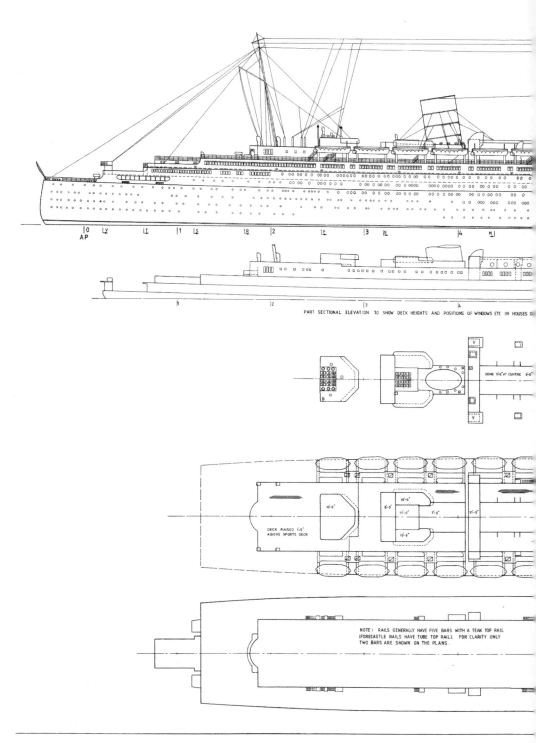

PART SECTIONAL ELEVATION TO SHOW DECK HEIGHTS AND POSITIONS OF WINDOWS ETC IN HOUSES O

DOME 1'-6" AT CENTRE 9'-0"

DECK RAISED 1'-9"
ABOVE SPORTS DECK

NOTE : RAILS GENERALLY HAVE FIVE BARS WITH A TEAK TOP RAIL
(FORECASTLE RAILS HAVE TUBE TOP RAIL). FOR CLARITY ONLY
TWO BARS ARE SHOWN ON THE PLANS.

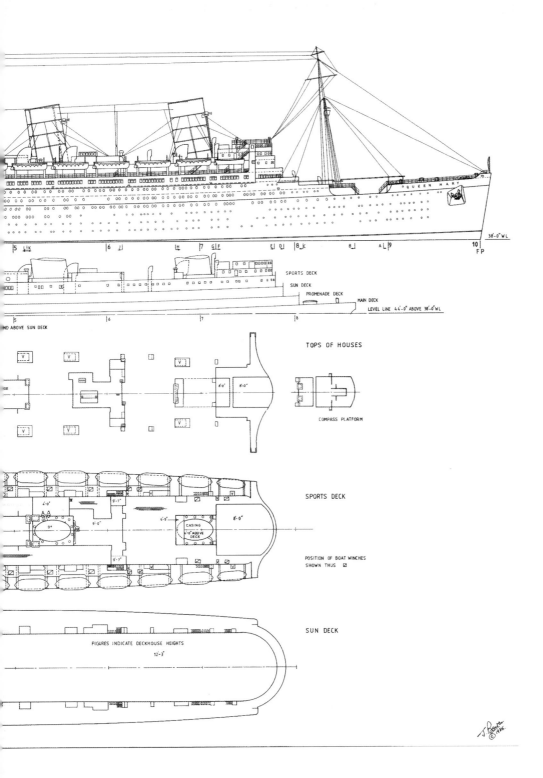

TOPS OF HOUSES

COMPASS PLATFORM

SPORTS DECK

POSITION OF BOAT WINCHES
SHOWN THUS ☑

SUN DECK

FIGURES INDICATE DECKHOUSE HEIGHTS

Queen Mary (1936) Cunard White Star Line

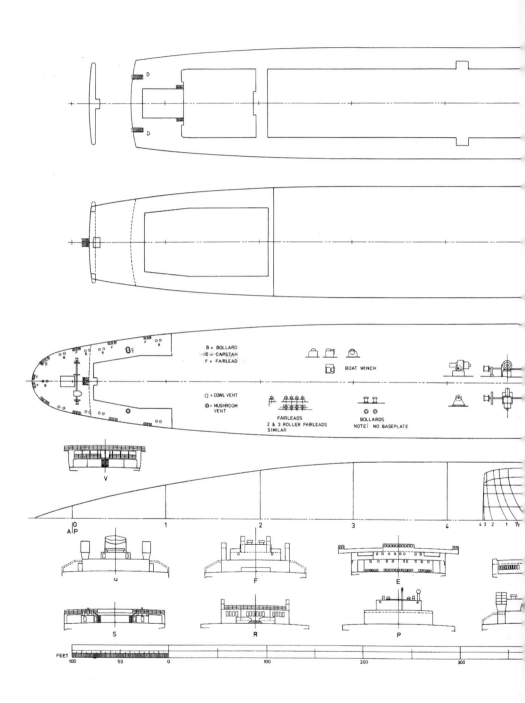

B = BOLLARD
C = CAPSTAN
F = FAIRLEAD

BOAT WINCH

C] = COWL VENT

Ⓜ = MUSHROOM
VENT

FAIRLEADS
2 & 3 ROLLER FAIRLEADS
SIMILAR

BOLLARDS
NOTE: NO BASEPLATE

V

10
A|P   1   2   3   4   43 2 1 1½

U   F   E

S   R   P

FEET   100   50   0   100   200   300

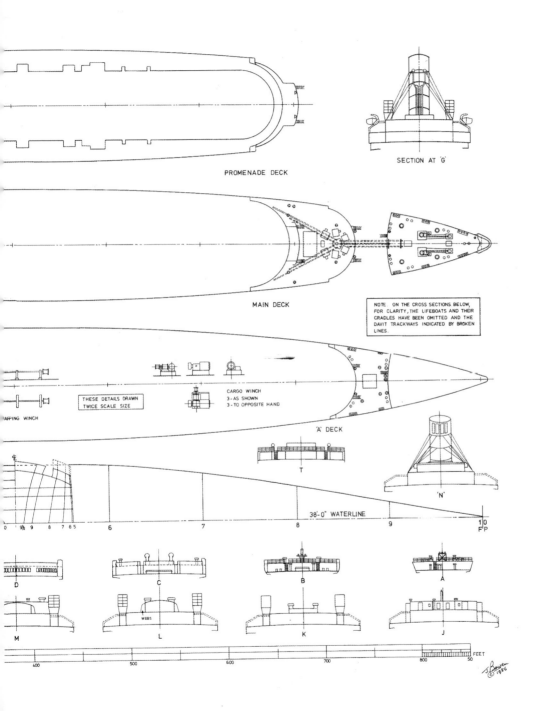

PROMENADE DECK

SECTION AT 'G'

MAIN DECK

NOTE: ON THE CROSS SECTIONS BELOW, FOR CLARITY, THE LIFEBOATS AND THEIR CRADLES HAVE BEEN OMITTED AND THE DAVIT TRACKWAYS INDICATED BY BROKEN LINES.

THESE DETAILS DRAWN TWICE SCALE SIZE

CARGO WINCH
3 - AS SHOWN
3 - TO OPPOSITE HAND

'A' DECK

WARPING WINCH

T

'N'

38'-0" WATERLINE

0 9½ 9 8 7 6 5   6   7   8   9   10
                                                                F.P

D   C   B   A

M   L   K   J

WEBS

400   500   600   700   800   50 FEET

Queen Mary under way – an impressive sight.

Cable lifters, cable trays, anchors: black.
Capstans: white.
Winches: black.
Bollards, fairleads: black.
Hatches: black coamings, white tops.
Funnels: Cunard red (Humbrol 174), black top, three narrow black bands.
Decks: all wood planked (Burma teak); tops of houses on Sports Deck and top of funnel casings grey (Humbrol 126).
Miscellaneous: inside bulwarks white.

References

The Cunard White Star Quadruple Screw Liner Queen Mary, which is a facsimile reprint of the 1936 souvenir issue of the technical journal *The Shipbuilder & Marine Engine-Builder* (Patrick Stephens Ltd, 1972); *The Cunard Liner Queen Mary* by Ross Watton in the 'Anatomy of the Ship' series (London: Conway Maritime Press, 1989); *RMS Queen Mary – 50 Splendid Years* by David Hutchings (Southampton: Kingfisher Railway Productions, 1986).

The technical journals *Shipbuilding & Shipping Record, Shipping World* and *Engineering* covered the construction and completion of the ship in various issues between 1930 and 1936 and included a number of small-scale general-arrangement plans.

Photographs: the Scottish Record Office (see Appendix II, pp205–206) holds a good range of shots of the vessel under construction and fitting out afloat; many specialist maritime photograph suppliers and agencies have the ship in their lists.

Plans: many of the shipbuilder's plans of the ship are held by Glasgow University Archives & Business Records Centre (see Appendix II); Harold Underhill produced a set of scale drawings of the ship, details of which are available from Brown, Son & Ferguson, Glasgow (see Appendix II, pp205–206).

SOURCES

Materials

Most materials can be found in model shops or art and craft shops. For entomological pins contact Watkins & Doncaster Lt (PO Box 5, Cranbrook, Kent TN18 5EZ).

Plans

The Shipbuilding Industry – A Guide to Historical Records, edited by L A Ritchie (Manchester: Manchester University Press, 1992) is a very useful guide to any archive material, including ship plans, that is still in existence following the closure over the past 150 years of the once numerous shipyards in this country.

Some archives may hold plans for shipyards other than those listed below. Where the plans from a particular yard are shown in more than one archive, generally they are for different periods in the company's existence. Few collections contain plans of all the ships built at a particular yard, and those for individual ships vary from very comprehensive sets of general arrangements, rigging, lines and other plans to just a few oddments.

City of Dundee District Council, Archive & Record Centre (21 City Square, Dundee DD1 3BY) hold plans of Gourlay Bros & Co, Dundee, and of the Caledon Shipbuilding & Engineering Co Ltd, Dundee.

Glasgow City Archives (Mitchell Library, North Street, Glasgow G3 7DN) hold plans from the Fairfield Shipbuilding & Engineering Co Ltd, Glasgow (mainly of ships built the 20th century).

Glasgow University Archives and Business Records Centre (13 Thurso Street, Glasgow G11 6PE) holds many plans from a number of Clyde shipyards including: The Ailsa Shipbuilding Co Ltd, Troon; John Brown & Co Ltd, Clydebank; Fleming & Ferguson Ltd, Paisley; Greenock Dockyard Co Ltd, Greenock; Wm Hamilton & Co Ltd, Port Glasgow; Lithgows Ltd, Port Glasgow; Scotts' Shipbuilding & Engineering Co Ltd, Greenock; Alexander Stephen & Sons Ltd, Glasgow.

The National Maritime Museum (Greenwich, London SE10 9NF) holds a very large collection of plans of ships of all types and periods, including naval vessels. Among these are plans from shipyards such as: Barclay, Curle & Co Ltd, Glasgow; Wm Denny & Brothers Ltd, Dumbarton; Fairfield Shipbuilding & Engineering Co Ltd, Glasgow (principally those for ships built between 1870 and 1895); R & W Hawthorn, Leslie & Co Ltd, Newcastle upon Tyne; Lithgows Ltd, Port Glasgow; Smith's Dock Co Ltd, South Shields; Swan, Hunter & Wigham Richardson Ltd, Newcastle upon Tyne; John I Thornycroft & Co Ltd, Southampton; Vickers-Armstrong Ltd, Barrow-in-Furness and Newcastle-upon-Tyne; J Samuel White & Co Ltd, Cowes, Isle of Wight.

The Science Museum Library (South Kensington, London SW7 5NH) can be contacted for back issues of many technical journals (and also contains a photocopy section).

Smithsonian Institution, Division of Transportation (Room 5101, Washington DC20560, USA) holds plans of American merchant ships.

Tyne & Wear Archives (Blandford House, Blandford Square, Newcastle upon Tyne NE1 4JA) contains many plans from a number of North East Coast shipyards.

The Ulster Folk & Transport Museum (Holywood, Northern Ireland BT18 0EU) holds the Harland & Wolff collection of ships' plans; however no copies of these plans are available either from the museum or from the yard itself. The Museum also holds that yard's collection of photographs and it is possible to obtain copies of these.

University of Liverpool Cunard Archives (PO Box 147, Liverpool L69 3BX) holds all Cunard records and plans.

Plans for ship modellers

Brown, Son & Ferguson Ltd (4/10, Darnley Street, Glasgow G41 2SD) can also be contacted for copies of the Harold Underhill range of plans of sailing ships and powered vessels.

David MacGregor Plans (12 Upper Oldfield Park, Bath, Avon BA2 3JZ) offer plans of a variety of vessels: sail and steam, merchant and naval.

Taubman Plans International (11 College Drive, Jersey City, New Jersey, NJ 07305 USA) can provide plans for ship modellers on a wide range of craft of all types and periods from many countries.

Photographs

The Imperial War Museum (Lambeth Road, London SE1 6HZ) holds warship photographs along with those of a number of merchant ships.

John Clarkson (18 Franklands, Longton, Preston, Lancashire PR4 5PD) has some merchant ship photographs, and also a few warship photographs.

Maritime Photo Library (8 Jetty Street, Cromer, Norfolk NR27 9HF) can be contacted for help in securing photographs of a variety of types and periods of vessel.

The National Maritime Museum (Greenwich, London SE10 9NF) contains a large collection of photographs of ships of all types.

Skyfotos/FotoFlite (Chart Road Industrial Estate, Ashford, Kent TN23 1ES) offer aerial photographs of ships, taken mainly in the English Channel.

Technical journals and magazines

Willens Press Guide is a valuable source for details of currently published magazines and papers on all manner of subjects, including shipping, shipbuilding and ship modelling, both in this country and worldwide. A copy can be found in the reference section of most public libraries.

In the following list those marked with an asterisk (*) are no longer in print, but copies can be found in a number of leading reference libraries:

The Motor Ship (1920)
* *The Shipbuilder* later *The Shipbuilder & Marine Engine-Builder* (1906)
* *Shipbuilding & Shipping Record* (1913)
Shipping World now *Shipping World & Shipbuilder*
* *Syren & Shipping*
The Engineer (1856)
Engineering (1866)
Note: these last two journals, because of their early foundation dates, frequently contain much useful information, often with plans, of contemporary merchant ships and naval vessels.
Hansa (Germany, 1864)
Schiff und Hafen (Germany, 1948)
Holland Shipbuilding (Holland, 1952)
Journal de la Marine Marchande (France, 1919)

The following current magazines are helpful for names and addresses of suppliers of ship modelling materials and equipment, new and second-hand maritime booksellers, ship photographs, ship model clubs, etc. Similar periodicals are published in other countries:

Sea Breezes
Ships Monthly
Shipping Today & Yesterday
Marine Modelling International
Model Shipwright
Model Boats
Le Modele Reduit de Bateau (France)
Modell Werft (Germany)
Model Ship Builder (USA)

INDEX